The Drawing of this Love

ROBERT FRUEHWIRTH

The Drawing of this Love

CANTERBURY
PRESS
Norwich

© Robert Fruehwirth 2016

First published in 2016 by the Canterbury Press Norwich

Editorial office
3rd Floor, Invicta House
108–114 Golden Lane
London EC1Y 0TG, UK

Canterbury Press is an imprint of Hymns Ancient & Modern Ltd
(a registered charity)

13A Hellesdon Park Road, Norwich,
Norfolk NR6 5DR, UK

www.canterburypress.co.uk

British Library Cataloguing in Publication data

A catalogue record for this book is available
from the British Library

Image on page 35: Crucifix, Master of San Francesco Bardi,
14th century, Galleria degli Uffizi, Florence

978 1 84825 836 5

Typeset by Regent Typesetting
Printed and bound in Great Britain by
CPI Group (UK) Ltd, Croydon

Contents

Introduction

A Quiet Day in London

Early one Saturday morning in October 2014, I was sitting in a room at the Royal Foundation of St Katharine's, a retreat and conference space in East London. I had come from Norwich to lead a quiet day of prayer and reflection for St Paul's Cathedral; Julian of Norwich, the great fourteenth-century mystic and theologian, was the focus of the day, with special regard to her most famous words: 'All shall be well.' As my train had arrived early, and the taxi had been quick (both miracles of God?), I'd arrived with time for a moment of quiet to myself before the day began.

Speaking on Julian was nothing new to me. For over 25 years I had read and prayed with Julian's *Revelations of Divine Love*, first as a monk in a monastic community devoted to her, then as a therapist, and finally as the priest director of the Julian Centre, next to the Julian Shrine in Norwich, a pilgrimage site that attracts visitors from all over the world.

I knew also from experience how powerful Julian's most well-known words, 'All shall be well', could be, not merely as the unofficial Julian motto, printed on everything from devotional cards to coffee mugs, and used in countless sermons, but as a phrase that somehow allowed people to let go of fear, even in the middle of seemingly unbearable crises.

One woman, on pilgrimage to the Julian Shrine, related how a friend had spoken 'all shall be well' to her while she was in intensive care in hospital. She knew almost nothing else about Julian, but just hearing this phrase, and allowing it into herself, had provided her with a doorway out of anguish into peace, even as she faced the possibility of death. I'd witnessed this effect of 'all shall be well' again and again. For some people these words actually effect what they say: they make people inwardly well again.

As I prepared for that day of reflection in London, I knew, however, that I wanted to do more than offer 'all shall be well' simply as a consoling promise. I also needed to share the profound challenge I found in 'all shall be well', and in Julian's spiritual vision as a whole, and the costly transformation that is required if we are to live into that vision.

As I confessed my lifelong struggle with 'all shall be well' with the gathered retreatants, and invited them to consider the trusting openness to all things that the phrase invites – to *all* of ourselves, and to *all* of life, and to *all* of the world's history as subject to God's well-making – a marvellous if bracing thing happened. Some in the group broke the assumed silence of the day, and, right in the middle of my talk, objected to what I was saying, sharing their fear of the radical acceptance and trust that 'all shall be well' invites. God might be entirely open to all that we are and all that we experience, and eager to make all our lives well, but could we risk being so open to ourselves, others and our world? Would this even be a good thing to do?

Without even bringing up the larger question of how God could make well the tragedies of world history, some confessed to feeling that their lives had already been hurt so badly by personal trauma that it seemed better *not* to open these to God in the hope that God could make them well. It seemed better to keep these locked away from the rest of an otherwise good life, better to live with a managed illness than to risk the pain of an actual cure. Others doubted that their difficult life experiences could ever be redeemed by love.

Such candour allowed us to get behind religious and spiritual clichés, and to question the very possibility of a spiritual life that touched all of ourselves and all of our world – the very possibility of living in real contact with a God of love who cherished all of us and could make all well. I knew the group's fear very well from my own experience, and in challenging 'all shall be well' together and probing its possibility, we were in very good company: Julian herself had argued with God through many chapters of the *Revelations*, insisting that the depth of suffering that she saw in the world could never be made well.

By the end of the day, toiling together in discussion and prayer, we came to the feeling that, even if we could not imagine how everything could be made well, we could in fact accept more of ourselves and the world into our awareness, and accept too God's promise of a love to make all things well, and at least allow ourselves, the world and God to be present within us. Just holding open this space where God's promise of love could be, along with our actual life experience, without having to work out how they fitted together, felt like a release into a new and deeper possibility for living: more in touch with ourselves, more open to the world in compassion, more receptive to God's working in love.

A Drawing of Love, a Journey of Faith

This book aims to share something of what happened on that quiet day and seeks too that place of exploration and developing faith where we can be more open to ourselves and our world, and to God, as Julian herself explores this in her *Revelations of Divine Love*. I want to accompany my readers as we face challenges in trying to live with this kind of faithful openness, not the least of which is the ongoing resistance to God that is in ourselves, and that becomes more apparent the closer we draw to God's reality.

Such honesty about our experience, in the face of spiritual and religious promises, is key, since so often spiritual language, inspiring for a moment, fails to connect with real life and leaves us only more empty and more self-doubting. Julian herself is an ideal model for such honesty and even objection in the face of religious ideas. Not only does Julian present us in her *Revelations* with a compelling vision of a God of love, compassionately at work in all things, but she is honest about how *hard* it was for her to accept a God who loved and worked in this way, how she rebelled against it, withdrew from it and argued against it. As we read the *Revelations*, we are thus encouraged by Julian's example to be honest in ourselves and with each other about what it is like to encounter such profound beliefs about God and attempt to make them our own.

The title of this book thus describes exactly what it is about. On the one hand, it is about Julian's revelation of God, who draws us in love into Godself and is at work, now and always, to make all things well. On the other hand, it is about the growth in faith that we undergo in learning to trust in God's love, to pray through our stubborn resistance to it and to open ourselves increasingly to its healing.

The Focus of this Book: Not Julian but Our Faith

Apart from a brief introduction to Julian, and occasional reference to her historical context, Julian herself, or the *Revelations of Divine Love*, are not the primary focus of this book.

Its focus is rather the life of faith in ourselves – its nature, its practical development and its fruition in ordinary life. I trust that we will in fact learn a great deal about Julian and her writings as we read through her *Revelations*, but I hope even more that we will gain a new clarity and confidence about engaging our Christian faith. It might sound paradoxical, but the chief pastoral aim in reflecting on divine love as Julian presents it might well be to make us keenly aware of all that is least loving and least loved in ourselves, so that these parts of ourselves can be seen accurately, understood, and allowed into the process of God's healing.

Not making Julian herself the focus is, I think, just as Julian would have it. She did not want her readers to become fascinated by her or her experiences as ends in themselves. She chose rather to maintain her anonymity, and she wanted her readers to see *themselves* as the subject of the spiritual experiences that she records in her *Revelations*, as if God wanted to give each of us the same revelation of love. As Julian wrote:

I beg you all for God's sake, and advise you for your own benefit, that you disregard the wretch to whom [the revelation of divine love] was shown, and with all strength, wisdom and humility contemplate God, who in his courteous love and unending goodness wished to make it generally known, to the comfort of us all. For it is God's will that you receive [the revelation] with joy and delight as great as if Jesus had shown it to you all. (BW, LT 8)

Without minimizing Julian's historical importance and the marvellous scholarship being done on her, it is still possible, as this book intends, to approach her writings principally as prayer, opening us more deeply to God and to ourselves.

The Structure of this Book: the Shape of Our Journey

The structure of this book traces Julian's own difficult process as she attempts to respond to God. It follows Julian's description of her mystical experience in what is known as the 'Long Text', the mature version of her *Revelations*. This long version includes most of Julian's original account of her experience of God, but adds 20 years of reflection and the fruits of her life of prayer. Such a multilayered text, offering the story of a personal spiritual experience and two decades of ensuing reflection, is offered by few spiritual writers, but such richness also makes for complexity.

Some parts of the *Revelations* relate one vivid experience of God after another in almost breathless succession (as in Mark's Gospel, event is piled on event without any time to digest them). Other parts contain reflections stretching for several chapters, without any obvious relationship to a particular mystical experience. There are also significant sections where Julian is intent on summarizing the meaning of her revelations and offering practical counsel to her readers.

Happily, by following the general structure of Julian's *Revelations* themselves, we end up with a structure appropriate for reflecting on our growing in faith.

In Part One of this book, 'Julian's Experience: A Showing of Love and the Emergence of Faith', we cover the initial 12 Showings and the initial 26 chapters of the *Revelations*. In this section we remain very close to the personal story and mystical experience that Julian had in 1373. We explore Julian's direct experience of God and what it tells us about the nature of her faith and the challenge it makes to us as we seek to make this our own.

In Part Two, 'Julian's Questioning: The Critical Testing and Deepening of Faith', we enter a strikingly different kind of terrain as we journey through Chapters 27–51 of the *Revelations*, in which Julian critically questions what she has already experienced, and struggles for a more coherent understanding. There are only two new Showings in this second part of the *Revelations*, but these chapters contain some of Julian's richest psychological, therapeutic and theological reflection.

In Part Three, 'Julian's Counsel: Wisdom and Imagery for the Journey of Faith', we explore the remaining chapters of the *Revelations*, Chapters 52–86, which contain two final Showings but consist largely of Julian's meditations on the Christian experience of God and of the spiritual life more generally. This part of the *Revelations* also contains the bulk of Julian's advice to those seeking to live a life of faith in response to a God of love.

In a book of this length we can't give full attention to every passage of Julian's *Revelations*. Some choice and arrangement of passages remains necessary. I have taken more liberty in Parts Two and Three, summarizing longer passages and arranging them for the best sequence in our reflections. My aim has been always to remain as close to Julian as possible, so that the reader can feel they are in fact accompanying Julian through her text; but I wanted to make sure that neither myself nor the reader got lost in the sometimes complex interweaving of themes in a text that Julian laboured on for over two decades.

I have chosen to use Barry Windeatt's new translation of Julian, *Julian of Norwich: Revelations of Divine Love*, published by Oxford University Press in 2015. It is a delightful translation that is bound to become a standard in the years to come. At times

I have also made use of the translation by the Revd John-Julian Swanson OJN, *A Lesson of Love*, published by Walker and Co. in 1988, as I have used this translation personally for years and it is inevitably how I hear Julian's words in my mind. For the reader who wishes to read more of Julian in any translation – or in the original Middle English, which is not very difficult – I have referred to all passages from Julian's *Revelations* by the number of the chapter in which they fall, as well as the particular translation that the passage comes from. Almost all of these passages are from the Long Text of Julian's *Revelations*, but in a couple of instances where I have quoted from the earlier Short Text, this is explicitly noted. Also, in order to avoid any confusion, I refer to Julian's text as a whole as the *Revelations*, and I refer to each individual revelation, of which there are 16, using Julian's medieval word of *Showing*. Thus we have Showing 1, Showing 2 and so forth, up to Showing 16, in Julian's *Revelations*.

A Journey of Faith, a Journey towards Wholeness

Julian insists, over and over again, that God draws us into God-self by drawing us into a wholeness and wellness in ourselves, and this wholeness, with its attendant openness to God, is something we are then invited to embody, and enact, in ordinary life. We make the journey of faith with Julian through her *Revelations*, so that God can establish new habits of trust and compassion in us: compassionate tenderness towards ourselves, one another, and even towards God, whom Julian saw as desiring us and our loving response.

> I saw that God is our true peace, and our sure protector when we are not at peace in ourselves, and he works continually to bring us into endless peace. And so when we, through the working of mercy and grace, are made humble and gentle, we are completely safe. Suddenly the soul is united to God when it is truly at peace in itself, for no anger is to be found in God. (BW, LT 49)

With the drawing of this Love and the voice of
    this Calling
We shall not cease from exploration
And the end of all our exploring
Will be to arrive where we started
And know the place for the first time ...

And all shall be well and
All manner of thing shall be well
When the tongues of flames are in-folded
Into the crowned knot of fire
And the fire and the rose are one.

T. S. Eliot, 'Little Gidding' V, *The Four Quartets*,
London: Faber & Faber, 2001

PART ONE

Julian's Experience:
A Showing of Love and the
Emergence of Faith

I

Julian's Desire for Three Gifts from God

Who Was Julian of Norwich?

We know very little for certain about Julian of Norwich herself. Scholars have debated inconclusively for decades about her background, while historical sleuths have offered various hypotheses about her identity and early life. Some believe that she came from a wealthy family, others suggest that she had been a Benedictine nun living in a convent in Norwich. Several authors suggest that Julian had been a wife and mother, who lost her husband and children early in life, perhaps in one of the waves of the Black Death that swept through Europe in the fourteenth century.

One thing we do know is that, some time in her adulthood, probably after she was 30 years old, Julian became an *anchorite* at St Julian's Church in Norwich. An anchorite was a person, common in medieval England, who took vows that consecrated them to a life of austerity, prayer and offering spiritual counsel. They were thus like monks and nuns, except that they lived not in convents or monasteries but alone, in solitude, in small apartments attached usually to a parish church.

A great deal of the problem in tracking who Julian was goes back to the likelihood that when she became an anchorite at St Julian's Church, she stopped using her baptismal and family name and took as her own that of the patron saint of the parish church where she became an anchorite. The church where Julian lived as an anchorite was thus not named after her, but after St Julian of Le Mans or perhaps St Julian Hospitaller, centuries before Julian herself got there. When she took the name 'Julian' from the church, as it is almost certain that she did, she effectively shrouded her earlier life in anonymity. As a result, we know nothing for certain about Julian other than what she relates in her *Revelations*, and from a handful of other sources, such as existing wills that leave money for her maintenance as an anchorite.

From these sources we can gather that Julian was born around 1342. We know also that she lived at least until 1416, perhaps longer. We know that she had at least two lay-sisters who took care of her needs. We also know, because Julian herself tells us, that when she was 30 years old, in May 1373, she underwent a series of experiences that she understood as direct experiences of God, commonly called *mystical experiences*, which became the source of all her later writing. These mystical experiences happened over a couple of days and nights and Julian organized them into sixteen different *Showings*. We can surmise from Julian's own description that she became an anchorite some time after this.

As to her writings, we currently possess both a 'Short Text' and versions of a 'Long Text' of what is now commonly known as *The Revelations of Divine Love*. Most Julian scholars agree that the Short Text was written shortly after Julian's mystical experiences, as it is a brief, autobiographical account of her experience of God. Around six times longer, the Long Text appears to have been written between 15 and 20 years later, and includes most of the Short Text, with significant amounts of theological reflection and pastoral counsel woven in. The Long Text is what people commonly read when they read Julian of Norwich's *Revelations of Divine Love*.

Julian's Youthful Desire for Three Gifts

As we turn to Julian's *Revelations*, we find that Chapter 1 is a table of contents, probably written by a scribe, which provides a short description of each of the 16 Showings.

In Chapter 2 we encounter Julian herself, beginning to share her experience of God. Here Julian describes herself as desiring, in her youth, three particular gifts of God. She tells us quickly what these three gifts were:

> These revelations were shown to a simple, uneducated creature in the year of our Lord 1373, on the eighth day of May. This person had already asked for three gifts by the grace of God. The first was to relive his Passion in her mind; the second was bodily sickness; the third was that God would give her three wounds. (BW, LT 2)

A visionary experience of the Passion of Christ? A bodily sickness? Three wounds? Reading just this much, we are thrust into a devotional and spiritual landscape that seems alien to most of us. The young Julian is asking God actually to *re-live* Jesus' Passion, for a sickness taking her to the point of death, and for three 'spiritual wounds'.

Helpfully, Julian explains her desire for the each of the gifts:

> As for the first gift [Julian says], it seemed to me that I had some feeling for the Passion of Christ but I still wanted more ... I wished I had been there at that time with Mary Magdalene and with others who loved Christ, so that I might have seen with my own eyes the Passion which our Lord suffered for me, and so that I might have suffered with him as others did who loved him. And so I longed for a vision of him in the flesh, by which I might have more knowledge of the bodily sufferings of our Saviour and of the fellow-suffering ... of all those who truly loved him ... I wanted to have afterwards a truer perception of Christ's Passion. (BW, LT 2)

Such a request for a vision of the Passion of Christ is perhaps not so strange after all. The Church regards meditation on the Passion of Christ as standard Christian practice, particularly during Lent and Holy Week. In order to come to grips with the mystery of Jesus and his death, we might, for instance, read the Gospel accounts of the Passion, or listen to music inspired by it, or contemplate artwork and iconography depicting Jesus' death. In her first desire, Julian wants the same kind of contact with the reality of Christ's death that we might have in ordinary devotion, but she wants to have it as directly and as keenly as possible; through an extraordinary religious experience she wants to re-live it. Julian feels that such an experience would allow her to be faithful and loving.

The second gift that Julian seeks, she says, is a sickness, 'severe enough as to seem mortal, so that in that illness I might receive all the rites of Holy Church, myself believing that I was to die' (BW, LT 2). Julian is not seeking a near-death experience in the modern sense of the term, as an experience of going beyond the grave in order to touch something of heaven. Rather, Julian wants to go right up to the brink of death and expect to die, yet still live. She tells us that she wanted this so as to be 'purged by the mercy of God, and afterwards live more to the glory of God'.

Like her first request, this seems extreme at first, but on reflection it is not so removed from contemporary experience. It is almost a commonplace for people to say that their lives have been transformed by a brush with death, becoming more compassionate, for instance, following a nearly fatal car accident. Having an awareness of death often allows us to engage life more thoughtfully and consciously, more in touch with ourselves and deeper values. In the same way, Julian is seeking to be 'purged' of vain preoccupations to live more truly, more to 'the glory of God'.

Julian's third request is for three spiritual gifts or graces, which she characterizes as *wounds*: 'the wound of true contrition, the wound of kind compassion, and the wound of purposeful longing for God' (BW, LT 2). In these wounds Julian is seeking to be more transparent with herself before God, to be more compassionately in touch with God and others and to have a greater desire for and sense of belonging to God.

But why does Julian use the metaphor of 'wounds' to speak of these things? In the Short Text, Julian tells us that she was inspired by the example of an early Christian martyr, St Cecilia, who suffered three neck wounds before she died (BW, ST §1). Even with this devotional precedent in her mind, it is still curious that Julian conceived of contrition, compassion and longing as coming to her as wounds, opened up by blows from the outside, rather than as qualities that might emerge from within her. This tells us something perhaps about Julian's youthful spirituality: while she desired intensely to live in loving faithfulness to God, she was frustrated in her desire to do so. Unable to live as she deeply desired, stuck and unable to make the spiritual progress she wanted, she felt as though violence had to be done to her from outside, in an extraordinary divine intervention, in order for her to live more in touch with her own truth and God's reality. The sense of being stuck spiritually, of being unable to live as we'd like, is common in Christian experience from St Paul onwards.

Interestingly, Julian tells us that while the desire for the first two gifts 'passed from my mind ... the third [that is, the desire for the three wounds] remained with me continually' (BW, LT 2).

Intimations of the Journey We Have Already Begun

Julian does in fact receive all three of these gifts in the course of the mystical experiences recorded in the *Revelations*: the 16 Showings happen for Julian in the context of a near-death; they are centred initially on the suffering of Jesus in his Passion; and, finally, the Showings allowed contrition, compassion and purposeful longing for God to emerge as powerful and orientating forces in Julian's life. We might say that because of her mystical experiences, Julian became more truthful and self-acceptant, more empathically in touch with herself, others and God, and that her desiring was more gathered into a desire for God.

As we begin our walk with Julian, her three youthful desires show us something about the kind of journey that we are about to undertake with Julian as our guide.

First, we are going to spend some time with the physical suffering and death of Jesus of Nazareth as revealing something about ourselves and God's presence and action in our lives. Julian's experience of Jesus' Passion, and our experience with her, will be fundamentally a prolonged journey into the mystery of compassion: God's compassion for us, and ours for God and one another.

Second, just as Julian gained perspective on life, and wisdom, by suffering a sickness in which she thought she was going to die, in the journey of this book we are going to step back from everyday concerns in order to attempt to see life more holistically, and to ask the biggest possible questions about our lives, our faith, our hope. What we are after is clarity about the most basic purpose and direction of our lives.

Third, Julian's use of the metaphor of 'wounds' reminds us that when qualities of soul such as truthfulness, or compassion, or love begin to emerge in us, we might well experience these as a wounding of our otherwise 'strong' selves. We might well experience such new spiritual qualities at first as a hurt vulnerability that yet allows, over time, a more substantial contact with ourselves, others and God.

The seventeenth-century poet John Donne famously asked God to break open his soul to God's presence and rule:

Batter my heart, three-personed God, for you
As yet but knock, breathe, shine, and seek to mend;
That I may rise and stand, o'erthrow me, and bend
Your force to break, blow, burn, and make me new.

For some of us, to know that we are beginning a journey with Julian that is going to 'break, blow, burn, and make us new' might feel like a relief. Finally, our small, closed-in hearts are going to be broken open to something larger. Our self-centredness and self-delusion are finally going to be pierced and undone. We might even surmise that the spiritual wounds we already have in our souls – the trauma, loss and pain we have already suffered in life – can become, through this journey of faith, the very experiences that allow for a more transparent, truthful and compassionate life, and a life more gathered into the desire for God.

Questions for Reflection and Discussion

At the end of each chapter in this book, I will offer questions for reflection and discussion, sometimes with suggestions for spiritual practice. The reader might want to find a small notebook in which she or he can write down notes about our reflections, as a record of our journey with Julian.

1 As you begin this journey with Julian through her *Revelations*, what are you seeking? What do you desire? Why have you picked up this book?
2 What do you think of, what images come to mind, when you imagine the Passion of Jesus? Can you imagine yourself standing with all of 'Christ's lovers' just as Julian did, at the foot of the cross? Do you in any way want to accompany Jesus in his death, to know what this was like for him? Why or why not?
3 Julian has shared with us her youthful desire for three gifts, which, through the *Revelations*, became the basis for her whole life's spiritual development and response to God. In the same way, our own youthful spiritual desires and religious experiences may tell us something of the essence of our spiritual truth and relationship with God. Can you remember your own youthful spiritual, religious or idealistic desires? How have these been frustrated or realized? How have they grown, or changed? How do you understand them now?
4 Julian imagines compassion as a spiritual wound. Take a moment to imagine compassion in your heart – compassion for yourself, compassion for a friend, compassion for a stranger, compassion even for an enemy. What does it feel like to offer another compassion?

2

Before the Beginning:
Julian's Sickness and Questioning

A Near-Death Illness

In the third chapter of Julian's *Revelations*, one of the most over-looked chapters in the book, Julian describes the onset of her near-death sickness that becomes the context for her mystical experiences.

It is worth stopping a moment to dwell on this chapter, because the near-death illness forces Julian, as only a near-death illness can, to struggle with the most fundamental questions about life and death, and what our basic orientation should be if we are to continue living.

She begins her third chapter by telling us about her bodily sickness.

> And when I was thirty and a half years old, God sent me a bodily sickness in which I lay for three days and three nights; and on the fourth night I received all the rites of Holy Church and did not expect to live until morning. (BW, LT 3)

She fully expects to die, and she receives the Last Rites of the Church, then understood as a final preparation for death. However, Julian thinks it sad to die so young:

> Being still young, I thought it was a great pity to die, but this was not because of anything on earth that I wanted to live for, nor because I was afraid of any pain, for I trusted in God's

mercy. But it was because I wanted to live so as to have loved God better and for longer, in order that I might, through the grace of that living, have more knowledge and love of God in the bliss of heaven. (BW, LT 3)

Julian's Desire for More Life

For Julian, the purpose of human life is to develop our capacity for knowing and loving God; we might say our capacity for relationship in general. Such development was charged with special meaning for Julian because the degree to which we grow into knowing and loving God in this life apparently determined for her our capacity to do so for all eternity. It's as if our eternal capacity for personhood, for love and truth and relationship, is determined by what we manage to grow into (or not) in this life.

Ruth Burrows, a contemporary spiritual writer from the Carmelite tradition, shares such a developmental view of the human person:

> A great insight of our times is that of man [and we might say, woman] becoming. Earlier generations conceived of the world and man as static. Man was there waiting to be explored ... Think of your soul as a castle, St. Teresa tells us, God dwells in the innermost room ... the rooms are there, it is just that you haven't learned to enter them. But nowadays we see things differently. The rooms are not there! We grasp that we are gradually coming into being; the potentiality that we are unique in each instance is slowly 'realized.' How can God dwell in depths that are not there as yet? (*Guidelines for Mystical Prayer*, pp. 9–10.)

Julian wants to live longer because she will have more chance of coming into what Burrows calls her 'potentiality'. Being faced with death as unavoidable, Julian, however, tells us that she surrenders to God this fate of dying young. Julian releases herself entirely to God's will and to her own death, even if this limits her *eternal* reality!

Compassion with Jesus in Ordinary Life

With this surrender, all seems settled – until Julian begins to feel better, and realizes that she is actually going to continue living. Thus, having already made a total surrender of herself to God, and disposed herself for death, feeling that she was going to live longer did not comfort her:

> [N]or did feeling more comfortable in this way fully comfort me, for it seemed to me I would rather have been released from this world, because my heart was willingly set upon that. (BW, LT 3)

In a way that many of us never experience, Julian had made a total surrender of herself to God at what she thought was the point of death, and thus released all ties with earthly life. Feeling better, however, she is aware of herself, hovering right on the edge of this life and about to re-enter it.

And it's here, right at this point of re-entering ordinary earthly life, that Julian remembers her youthful desire for the spiritual wound of compassion, and for a special experience of the Passion of Christ. These, she says, suddenly came to her mind:

> Then it suddenly came to mind that I ought to wish for the second wound [of compassion] as a gift and a grace from our Lord, so that my body might be filled with recollection and feeling of his blessed Passion, as I had prayed before; for I wanted his pains to be my pains, with compassion, and then longing for God. (BW, LT 3)

What happens next is wondrous. Julian realizes that she does not need an *extraordinary mystical or visionary experience* at all to realize compassionate intimacy with Jesus or to re-live his Passion. From the perspective of near-death, Julian sees that ordinary human life itself, living in 'a mortal body', if lived in surrender, is a way of being intimately one with Jesus and even of dying with him.

It seemed to me that, through his grace, I might have the wounds which I had wanted before. But in this I never asked for any bodily vision or any kind of revelation from God, but for compassion, such as it seemed to me a naturally sympathetic soul might feel for our Lord Jesus, who for love was willing to become a mortal man. And I longed to suffer with him, while living in my mortal body, as God would give me grace. (BW, LT 3)

Julian realizes that ordinary life could be experienced as compassionate union with Jesus, because Jesus out of love has already taken our experience of ordinary life into himself. It's as if the bridge into Jesus' reality is already there: it is our ordinary life.

A First Glimpse of Julian's Faith in Action

This sudden realization of Julian's – that she could have her long-sought intimacy and knowledge of God not through special visionary experience, but in living open and surrendered to God in ordinary life – is a first glimpse of what faith does: it takes human experience and makes that experience open to God, and an experience of increasing intimacy with God, and knowledge of God, who chooses to share our experience with us in Jesus.

The faith that Julian presents us with, on this very first glimpse, is thus not primarily about subscribing to certain beliefs, or having a vague trust in a 'God'. Still less does it mean being carried away into spiritual worlds or having special experiences. Yes, faith does involve believing things, faith does involve trust and faith does allow for certain experiences of God. But at its most essential level the practice of faith, as Julian understood it, means being open to the experiences we have had and the experience we are having in each moment as, at some level, already our openness to God: God sometimes suffering deep pain with us, and God sometimes transfigured with glory in our joy and delight.

Questions for Reflection and Discussion

1 Have you experienced anything like a near-death illness? Or have you experienced this in a lesser way, being with the death of another, for example, or being in hospital for weeks on end? What was it like to slip out of the normal pattern of life? What was it like to come back to ordinary life? Did you learn anything? Did your values change?

2 Julian conceives of compassion with Christ as occurring through her openness to ordinary human experience. Have you experienced moments where you have been able to be open to the present moment without any resistance at all, such as in moments of transcendent beauty, love or loss? Some people experience this before works of art, or in church, or in prayer. What has this been like for you?

3 Julian seems to assume that the purpose of life is to grow in our capacity for truth and love, for understanding and intimacy. Is this enough? Do you see this kind of growth as the purpose of your life? Or do we need to add something about actively and intentionally helping others?

3

A Revelation of God's Homeliness

Suffering Humanity and the Blissful Trinity

During her illness, Julian's curate came and held before Julian a crucifix, a visual representation of Jesus suffering on the cross. The curate invited Julian to gaze on this crucifix to comfort herself at the time of her dying.

> [The curate] set the cross before my face and said, 'I have brought you the image of your maker and Saviour. Look at it and take comfort from it.' (BW, LT 3)

Julian's mystical experience, the First Showing, begins as she gazes on this image of the dying Jesus and sees blood coming from under the crown of thorns that had been pressed on to his head:

> I suddenly saw [Julian says] the red blood trickling down from under the crown of thorns, hot and fresh, plentiful and lifelike, just as though it were the moment in his Passion when the crown of thorns was pressed on to his blessed head, he who was both God and man, the same who suffered for me in this way. (BW, LT 4)

I suddenly saw! The crucifix has come alive for her; Julian is suddenly having a visionary experience, seeing Jesus' Passion as though it were happening in front of her.

This is extraordinary enough, but Julian quickly adds a second dimension to her first Showing. In sharp contrast to her sight of the suffering humanity of Jesus, her heart is suddenly also filled with joy in God. As Julian says:

> And in the same revelation the Trinity suddenly filled my heart full of the utmost joy, and I understood that it will be like that in heaven forever for all those who will come there ... the Trinity is our maker, the Trinity is our protector, the Trinity is our everlasting lover, the Trinity is our unending joy and bliss (BW, LT 4)

Julian's *Revelations* thus begin with a double-layered vision. One layer is about the suffering humanity of Christ in his Passion. Because Jesus' suffering includes for Julian all the suffering of creation, this vision is also implicitly about Julian's own suffering and that of all human beings, included in the hurt body of Jesus. In sharp contrast to this, the second layer of the vision is about the eternal joy of the Trinity, unqualified and unconstrained, and this fills Julian with unconditional joy and bliss. In the very first instance of her mystical experience of God, Julian is thus simultaneously in touch with the vulnerability and suffering inherent in being human, as well as with a life of unconditional affirmation and security in God.

As we journey further with Julian, we will discover that this dual-layering of her awareness, simultaneously open to God and open to suffering self and world, is an essential characteristic of her spirituality. Utter security in God's joy and love seems always to be accompanied by a new vulnerability to our human experience, and these two arrive together in the person of Jesus.

As if to underscore the dual-layering of her first experience, Julian says that throughout the rest of the *Revelations*, whenever Jesus appears in his humanity, the whole Trinity is understood.

> [T]he Trinity is our unending joy and bliss, through our Lord Jesus Christ ... this was shown in the first [Showing] and in them all; for where Jesus appears, the blessed Trinity is to be understood. (BW, LT 4)

God's Homeliness: Julian's Delight and Assurance

Julian's initial response to this first Showing is not, however, to reflect on Jesus' suffering, or to wonder at the eternal joy of God. This will be the task of further Showings. Rather, what strikes Julian the most in this very first instance of the Showings is the fact that it is Jesus himself showing all this to her, that Jesus has chosen to be directly present to her, so intimate and self-sharing:

> I had a true and powerful perception that it was he himself who showed this to me without any intermediary ... And I said, 'Blessed be thou, Lord!' I said this with a reverent intention in a loud voice; and *I was much astounded at the wonder and amazement I felt, that he who is so much to be revered and so awesome was willing to be so friendly to a sinful being* ... (BW, LT 4, emphasis mine)

The word in Middle English that Julian uses to describe this directness and intimacy of Jesus to her, translated as 'friendly' in the passage above, is very special to her. It is the Middle English word *homeley*. *Homeley*, in Julian's time, meant friendly, simple, direct and lacking in pretence – intimate in a domestic kind of way. It also had connotations of gentleness, kindness and privacy, if not exactly secrecy.[1] *Homeley* evokes two friends sharing their inner selves and experience with each other simply, privately and honestly.

Julian's first response is thus to be awestruck, primarily because Jesus is being *homeley* with her, intimately and directly sharing with her his own reality.

As if to expand on this, Julian sees the Blessed Virgin Mary later in this same Showing as a kind of role model for this experience of divine homeliness. She writes:

> I saw [the Blessed Virgin Mary] in a spiritual manner ... in the form that she was when she conceived. God also revealed in

---

1 Source: ME Dictionary: http://quod.lib.umich.edu/cgi/m/mec/medidx?
type=id&id=MED21088.

part the wisdom and the truth of her soul, and in this I understood the reverent contemplation with which she beheld her
God who is her maker, marvelling with great reverence that
he was willing to be born of her who was a simple creature
of his making ... And this wisdom and faith, recognizing the
greatness of her maker and the littleness of her created self,
caused her to say very humbly to Gabriel, 'Behold me here, the
handmaid of the Lord.' (BW, LT 4)

Just as Mary felt awe and reverence that God would choose to
be born of her, so Julian feels awe and a sense of her own littleness at God's choice to be so intimate and familiar with her. The
feeling of littleness is important. Experiencing God's choice to be
homeley did not puff Julian up with self-importance. The feeling
seems to be more like the flush of joy we feel when someone we
admire chooses to share themselves with us.

So powerful is this experience of God's homely love that Julian
marks it out as the essence of the first Showing.

This vision [of the crown of thorns] was vivid and lifelike, and
horrifying and awesome, sweet and lovely. And what gave me
most comfort in the whole revelation that I saw was that our
God and Lord who is so much to be revered and so awesome is
so familiar [Middle English: *homeley*] and so courteous. *And
this is what most filled me with delight and assurance in my
soul.* (BW, LT 7, emphasis mine)

Delight and assurance! The vision of suffering might be horrible,
but Julian felt delight and assurance because of God's loving
homeliness. And such divine homeliness is meant not just for
Julian, but for all of us.

For truly it is the greatest possible joy, as I see it, that he who
is highest and mightiest ... is lowest and humblest, the most
friendly and the most courteous. And truly and indeed this
marvellous joy will be revealed to us all when we see him ...
the greatest fullness of joy that we shall have, as I see it, is the

marvellous courtesy and friendliness [that is, homeliness] of our Father who is our maker, in our Lord Jesus Christ who is our brother and our Saviour. But no one can know this marvellous intimacy in this life unless he receives it through a special revelation from our Lord, or through a great abundance of grace given inwardly by the Holy Spirit. (BW, LT 7)

Questions for Reflection and Discussion

1 Julian seems to locate heaven, and our delight and assurance, in the loving delight and homeliness of another, one whom we esteem highly. How have you experienced the loving gaze of another, one whom you esteem highly, and who delights in you? Can you remember what this was like? Can you imagine what it is like when a person you esteem highly decides to share herself or himself with you? Do you agree with Julian that such an experience does not inspire pride but makes you feel little, but delighted all the same?

2 The standard practices of the Church can be seen as ways of learning about and experiencing the closeness of God: reading Scripture, praying to God about our lives, engaging in worship together, sharing in Holy Communion, or practising silent contemplation, retreat and meditation. Where in your life have you been most aware of a God who is close to you? If you wanted to nurture this, is there one practice, more than the others, that you would give yourself to? Would you like to make yourself more available to God?

3 When Julian, and we, gaze on the suffering humanity of Jesus we are put in touch with our own suffering; we see our hurt selves in his hurt body. But we also see with Julian God's loving choice always to be close to us, and to accept all of our experience as God's own. We might also see, in the suffering Jesus, the systemic wrongness of so much of human society. Can you imagine seeing your own hurt in Jesus, that gazing on him in his Passion is a way of gazing

on your own Passion, or into the Passion of humanity suffering its own blindness and violence? Can you imagine Jesus
as a revelation of God's desire to be unconditionally open to
you in love? Can you then imagine addressing the Jesus who
is suffering? What would you say to him?

4

Hazelnuts, Clothing and
How We Pray

Introduction: The Richness of Showing 1

In the last chapter we reflected on the twofold nature of Julian's
first showing as revealing the essence of Julian's spirituality and
foreshadowing the kind of faith into which she is going to invite
us: journeying with Julian is going to mean becoming increasingly open to our humanity and, at the same time, open to God's
unconditional love. We reflected also on the awe Julian felt at
God's homely self-sharing, and the delight and assurance that
come from this.

In looking at these themes, we have, however, explored only
the first moment of the first Showing. As one of the most complex and vibrant of all the Showings, Showing 1 contains many
other elements – visions, images and reflections – that are some
of the most well-known and cherished in all of Julian's writings. It is therefore prudent to spend more time with Showing 1,
which Julian describes as the 'strength and foundation' (BW, LT
6) of all the *Revelations*.

God Is Our Clothing

Shortly after finishing her description of the double vision of
Jesus and the Trinity, Julian launches into a series of images that
are some of the most vivid in the *Revelations*. For the first time,
she begins to meditate explicitly on God's unconditional love for
us, and the metaphor that she deploys is that of *clothing*:

At the same time as I saw this vision of the head bleeding, our Lord showed me spiritually in a vision how intimately he loves us. I saw that [God] is to us everything that is good and comforting for our help. He is our clothing that out of love enwraps and enfolds us, embraces us and wholly encloses us, surrounding us for tender love, so that he can never leave us. And so in this vision I saw that he is everything that is good, as I understand it. (BW, LT 5)

Later in the Showing, Julian intensifies her metaphor for being enfolded in God, from that of clothing around us to the various, enclosing, physical layers of our own bodies:

For as the body is clad in cloth, and the flesh in the skin, and the bones in the flesh, and the heart in the chest, so are we, soul and body, clad and enclosed in the goodness of God. Yes, and more inwardly, for all these may decay and wear away. God's goodness is always complete, and incomparably closer to us, for truly our lover, God, wants our souls to cling to him with all their might, and always to be clinging to his goodness. (BW, LT 6)

Metaphors merge and spill over as Julian strives to communicate just how intimate, how totally enclosing, is her experience of God's goodness and love. Later in the *Revelations* she will say:

God is nearer to us than our own soul; for he is the foundation on which our soul stands, and he is the means that keeps the substance and the sensory being together, so that they will never separate; for our soul sits in God in true rest, and our soul stands in God in sure strength, and our soul is naturally rooted in God in endless love ... The noble city in which our Lord Jesus sits is our sensory being, in which he is enclosed. (BW, LT 56)

While the Church in Julian's time was preoccupied with a God of judgement and wrath, Julian offers a completely different sense of God: a God who is all that is good to us, who is tender, close, caring, and even maternal. There is no judgement in any of these images; there certainly is no wrath. This God does not send suffering to punish us, but joins us in tender solicitude in the inevitable suffering of our lives – sometimes intensified by sin – in order to make all of life, without conditions, the means by which we can grow spiritually. We ourselves are a *good creation*, in which God proudly sits for ever.

A Little Thing, the Size of a Hazelnut

A further vision of God's love, the most famous from all of the *Revelations*, follows on the image of God's goodness as our clothing. This is the image of all of creation held in Julian's hand as something little, something 'the size of a hazelnut'.

> [I]n this vision [God] showed a little thing, the size of a hazelnut, lying in the palm of my hand, as it seemed to me, and it was round as a ball. I looked at it with my mind's eye and thought, 'What can this be?' And the answer came in a general way, like this, 'It is all that is made.' I wondered how it could last, for it seemed to me so small that it might have disintegrated suddenly into nothingness. And I was answered in my understanding, 'It lasts, and always will, because God loves it; ... everything has its being through the love of God.' (BW, LT 5)

Here the love of God is taken to a metaphysical level, as the very ground of creaturely existence. God's love is not something conditional on good behaviour; it is rather the free choice of the creator God who loves us out of nothingness into being.

But there is something else here, and that is the near-nothingness of it all. As Julian wrote: 'it seemed to me so small that it might have disintegrated suddenly into nothingness' (BW, LT 5). Creation is fragile, it is almost nothing, it is about to fall away into nothingness. Part of Julian's spirituality involves seeing this near-nothingness, the contingency and fragility of created being, and thus seeing right through it to God.

Julian's First Conclusion: Setting All Things at Nought?

Julian first conclusion from this series of visions in Showing 1 is that nothing created can bring us to rest; only God can do this.

> It seemed to me that this little thing that is made [that is, creation] might have disintegrated into nothing because of its smallness. We need to know about this so as to delight in setting at nought everything that is made in order to love and possess God who is unmade. For this is the reason why we are not entirely at ease in heart and soul: because we seek rest here in these things which are so small and in which there is no rest, and do not know our God who is almighty, all wise, all good; for he is true rest ... When a soul has willingly made itself as nothing for love, in order to have him who is all, then he is able to receive spiritual rest. (BW, LT 5)

What does Julian mean by the idea of setting all things, even ourselves, at nought? This is not a methodical negating of one-self or a hatred of created things as a kind of purifying spiritual discipline. Rather, it is simply a matter of perspective. Just as Julian sees all of creation as something as small as a hazelnut *because she sees it in the context of a greater vision of God,* so she feels keenly that her heart can never be fully at rest in any-thing created because her heart at that moment is overfilled with the presence and joy and love of God. And, as we will see later in the *Revelations,* making ourselves 'nothing for love' in order to be with God entails not so much rigorous self-denial but, much more to the point, releasing what Julian calls our 'wrath', our resentment and anger at God's will and God's allowance for our lives.

Julian's Second Conclusion: Praying Directly to God

The second conclusion that Julian comes to in Showing 1 is about our way of prayer. If God is close to us, is homely and immedi-ate, good and loving, then our lives of prayer do not have to be especially complicated. We can approach God directly, trusting in God's goodness, and asking for all that we need:

> This revelation was given, as I understand it, to teach our souls the wisdom of clinging to the goodness of God ... Then I saw indeed that it is more honour to God, and more true delight, if we pray faithfully to God himself in his goodness and cling to that [goodness] by his grace, with true understanding and steadfast belief, than if we employ all the intermediaries that heart can devise. (BW, LT 6)

In Julian's time, people were used to praying to God through all kinds of intermediaries – through the saints, and through the veneration of holy objects and devotion to holy images. Julian says that, while we should use these intermediaries if they mediate God's goodness and love to us, we can nonetheless go straight before God in Godself. This should be the essence of our spiritual life: a radical, direct openness to God in Godself, trusting in God's goodness.

Contemplating God's goodness, and thus her ability to approach God in all simplicity, asking for God to give her God-self, Julian breaks out into prayer right in the middle of her narrative:

> God, of Thy goodness, give me Thyself; for Thou art enough to me, and I can ask nothing that is less that can be full honor to Thee. And if I ask anything that is less, ever shall I be in want, for only in Thee have I all. (JJS, LT 5)

The Contemplative Edge in Julian's Spirituality

Going straight before God, without thinking about the saints or holding before ourselves images of Jesus' humanity or reflecting on Scripture, is, however, to enter into a kind of mental darkness, because we have no adequate image or concept for God, or thought, or even specific feeling, to focus on. We have nothing to see, nothing finite to hold our attention, and with that our awareness spreads out into what can be described as a field-like awareness of presence and mystery. It is an experience of unknowing on one level and inchoate knowing on another.

Julian's sense of the near-transparency of creation before God (the hazelnut vision), and her being emboldened to go directly before God because of God's goodness and intimacy (the image of clothing), thus lead into what is commonly known as a contemplative spirituality of seeking for God in the apparent absence of creaturely images, words and intermediaries. All that is left to us is our naked desire for God, our need for God to care for us and our trust in God's presence.

Julian's spirituality has this contemplative element, yet it also celebrates devotion to the humanity of Jesus and the saints, and warmly embraces the free play of the religious imagination. The kind of faith we find in Julian is wonderfully broad as it is deep, almost ungoverned by specific spiritual methods. It does not constrain us to contemplative silence as *the necessary way to God*, as a kind of methodical spiritual programme, nor does it encourage only a devotion to the humanity of Jesus, or a necessity of staying with particular thoughts. Julian is extraordinarily free in engaging herself and God, and we can be too, in the images we have and also in going beyond such images because love urges us to.

Questions for Reflection and Discussion

1 Created Ways into God's Presence

If you were to attempt to 'set yourself in God's presence', or try to pray, how would you do this? Would you read a piece of Scripture, listening to it as God's word? Would you hold in your imagination an image of Jesus, perhaps teaching, or looking at you, or healing another, or suffering or in glory? Would you talk with him? Alternatively, would you attempt to let go of thoughts and images so as to rest in God's presence? Might remembering a friend who loves you, and the feeling you have with that person, be a way into God's presence?

Julian uses the metaphor of clothing to describe God's enfolding goodness; what metaphor would you use about how God is present or absent for you? What is God like: a voice that speaks love or judgement, a fire that burns and inspires, a river that runs through you, a thread that is followed?

2 Contemplative Spirituality

There are many teachers and methods of contemplative prayer and a contemplative way of life today. There is the Centring Prayer tradition taught by Basil Pennington, Thomas Keating and Cynthia Bourgeault, among others. There is the World Community for Christian Meditation started from John Main's teaching and continued now by Laurence Freeman, among others. Robert Llewelyn, Chaplain of the Julian Shrine, advocated a contemplative use of the Rosary. There also is the fourteenth century *The Cloud of Unknowing* and the Carmelite tradition of silence and unknowing in God's presence, found in the writings of John of the Cross.

Have you practised contemplative prayer, or silence, or emptiness of self, either formally or informally? What has this been like? Would you like to explore this more? See the Resources for Further Reading section at the end of this book.

5

Divinity Hidden in Our Humanity

Showing 2: Jesus' Hurt Body and Our Suffering

Having completed Showing 1, we begin a series of short, focused Showings – Showings 2 to 7. Each of these Showings is only one chapter long and each expands on one of the themes already encountered in Showing 1. Showing 2 begins with a bodily sight of the face of Jesus during his Passion:

> And after this [Julian says] I saw with my bodily sight in the face on the crucifix which hung before me – at which I was looking continuously – a part of his Passion: contempt, spitting and soiling, and blows, and many lingering pains, more than I can tell, and frequent changes of colour. (BW, LT 10)

Julian's initial vision of blood seeping out from under the crown of thorns is now expanded to include the whole face of Jesus, and an imaginative entry into his physical and psychological suffering.

> And once I saw how half his face, beginning at the ear, was caked with dry blood until it covered to the middle of his face, and after that the other half was covered in the same way, and meanwhile it vanished in the first part just as it had come. I saw this bodily, sorrowfully and dimly ... (BW, LT 10)

Such vivid imagery reminds us that Julian is not a systematic theologian, nor is she merely a devotional writer imagining

Jesus' death for her readers. She is in the first instance a mystic who is telling us what she saw.

Furthermore, we can imagine that in *seeing* Jesus' suffering in his face, the 'contempt, spitting and soiling, and blows, and many lingering pains', Julian is also seeing, at least implicitly, her own suffering, because, as noted above, Jesus' suffering is for Julian his suffering of our human experience. This is psychologically significant, devotionally powerful, and important for our journey with Julian. Gazing on Jesus in his Passion and into his death is an indirect, but psychologically powerful, way to gaze into our own Passions, already endured. The hurt of ourselves, of humanity and creation, sometimes unbearable and unapproachable, becomes more bearable when seen and touched first in the body of Jesus.

The Obscurity of this Vision

For Julian, the most significant part of this Showing is the fact that she can't see him clearly, the darkness and lack of clarity in her experience. She says:

> I saw this bodily, sorrowfully and dimly, and I wished for better bodily sight to have seen more clearly. And I was answered in my reason, 'If God wishes to show you more, he will be your light – you need none but him.' (BW, LT 10)

Julian can't see Jesus clearly, but she is reminded to trust in God to show her what she needs to see. There is something poignant here, on a devotional or even therapeutic level, about not being ready to face our suffering squarely, and of waiting for God to show us what we need to see. All through the *Revelations*, Julian presents God as inviting us into greater truthfulness, a clearer vision of exactly how things are, but wisely moderating what we can see and how we see it. For instance, Julian says that God shows us our sin only gradually and by 'the sweet gracious light of himself' (LT 78)

Julian takes this experience of not being able to see the vision as clearly as she'd like, and having to wait on God to show her more, in two different directions.

First she reflects on the general experience of seeking and finding God. Just as her vision of God is unclear in the second Showing, so Julian imagines that we are inchoately already in touch with God all the time.

Second, she reflects *theologically* on how God in love chose to take our human experience on fully, without constraints, and how this led to the glory of God in Jesus being hidden during his suffering.

These two different reflections converge once again on a theme that is central in Julian's faith: remaining open to our experience as a place where God always is, and is always offering Godself, especially in those times when any sense of the divine is obscured by suffering.

Seeking and Finding God

Julian says first that we only seek God insofar as we have some sight of the divine.

> [F]or we are now so blind and so unwise that we never seek God until out of his goodness he shows himself to us. And when we see anything of him by grace, then we are moved by the same grace to seek with great longing to see him more joyously. And so [Julian says] I saw him and sought him, and I had him and I wanted him. And this is, and should be, our usual way of proceeding in this life, as I see it. (BW, LT 10)

All our seeking of God is a result of already having found something of God, and wanting more. Seeing something of God wakes us up, arouses us and creates a desire for more vision.

> The seeking with faith, hope, and charity pleases our Lord, and the finding pleases the soul and fills it full of joy. And so I was taught in my understanding that seeking is as good as

beholding during the time that he will allow the soul to be at labour. (BW, LT 10)

Where Julian becomes radical is in her belief that we are always, already, seeking God in this life, which means that we must always be in touch with God in some way. Julian shares with us, in fact, pastoral advice that she receives from God, that it is helpful to us spiritually if we live with the assumption that we are already *seeing God continually*:

> For God wants us to believe that we see him continually, even though it seems to us that we see only a little, and through this belief he makes us to be gaining in grace continually. (BW, LT 10)

This is a crucial passage. Julian is telling us that God wants us to believe something: that we are seeing God continually, and that through this belief we will in fact grow in grace – grow, that is, in truthfulness and love, compassion and self-gift.

Julian is *not* presenting the notion of seeing God continually as a theological idea to be debated, whether or how God could have been present in this or that experience. Still less is she saying that, if we become pure enough, we can walk around in a perpetual experience of the divine.

No, she is saying something far more practical and down to earth: that it will be helpful to us if we approach our lives now with the belief, with the assumption, that God is already in this moment – not yesterday, not tomorrow, but this moment right in front of us. Practising this, we open ourselves to the present moment in the assumption that God is here, and that we are already seeing God.

De Caussade and the Sacrament of the Present Moment

Devotees of the seventeenth-century spiritual writer Jean-Pierre de Caussade, who made popular the notion of 'the sacrament of the present moment' and 'abandonment to divine providence', will note something similar between de Caussade and Julian's spirituality at this point. In both writers there is a link between the act of surrender to the reality of the present moment as the place where God already is, and thus being more open and responsive to God. In both it is a way of practising a faith in Jesus, as the God who comes to be with us in our humanity.

To say that the present moment is a sacrament, as de Caussade did, is to say that this moment in life is the outward and visible sign of an inward and spiritual communication of God's own life. For de Caussade, this was not a matter of always *feeling* that God was around, but was a practical spiritual assumption that allowed him to encounter the hard and painful facts of life differently, with more adeptness, creativity and grace. In his book *The Joy of Full Surrender* de Caussade wrote:

> There is not a moment in which God is not present with us under the cover of some pain to be endured, some obligation or some duty to be performed, or some consolation to be enjoyed. All that takes place within us, around us, or through us involves and conceals his divine hand. (Ch. 10)

> To be satisfied with the present moment is to delight in and to adore God's will in all that comes to us to do or suffer through the succession of events each passing moment brings ... Nothing hides him from the piercing eye of faith. The louder the sense exclaim, 'This cannot be from God!' the closer they press this bundle of myrrh from the hand of the Bridegroom ... *the life of faith is nothing less than the continued pursuit of God through all that disguises, disfigures, destroys and so to speak, annihilates him.* (Ch. 11, emphasis mine)

When we practise the presence of God in this moment, we are not thinking about *how* God could be present in this or that experience, but we approach life with the assumption that God is already present, and being open in that way. This is the work of faith.

The Theology: God's Hiddenness in Jesus

For Julian, the hiddenness of God within our suffering is repre-
sented in the person of Jesus, whose glorious and 'fair' divinity
was lost to sight, hidden under the suffering of his human experience. In Showing 2, Julian writes about this in terms of the
devotional tradition, popular during her time, of the 'holy
Vernicle in Rome'. This holy Vernicle was a cloth that was said
to have been pressed to Jesus' face during his Passion and still to
bear his imprint:

> [The suffering face of Jesus] made me think of the holy Vernicle
> in Rome, which he imprinted with his own blessed face while
> he was in his cruel Passion, willingly going to his death ...
> Many marvel how it could be – the brownness and blackness,
> the pitifulness and leanness of this image – considering that
> he imprinted it with his blessed face, which is the fairness of
> heaven, the flower of earth, and the fruit of the Virgin's womb.
> Then how could this image be so discoloured and so far from
> fair? (BW, LT 10)

Julian's answer is that love for us drove God to take all our
human experience into Godself, even our suffering, our violence
and our death. Thus the glory of Jesus' divinity was lost to sight
during his Passion:

> [F]or the love and honour of man, [God wanted] to make
> himself as like man in this mortal life, in our vileness and our
> wretchedness, as a man without sin could be ... it was the image
> and likeness of our foul, black, mortal covering, within which
> our fair, bright, blessed Lord God is hidden. (BW, LT 10)

What faith thus asks of us is a sustained openness to our present
experiencing as our way of remaining open and responsive to our
'fair, bright, blessed Lord' who is often hidden within the 'foul,
black, mortal covering' of our everyday experience. Growing in
faith doesn't mean necessarily experiencing the divine presence

more, but means growing in our ability to be open to varied experience as our way of sustained openness to God, even as an act of love and surrender to God. A great part of the rest of the *Revelations* is about how God helps us to do just this.

A Suggestion for Spiritual Practice and Reflection

The Sacrament of the Present Moment

Take a moment to stop now and bring your awareness into this present moment.

What does your body feel like from inside? Where do you feel the tension, aches and pains in yourself? Where is there energy, or the feeling of life and delight in you?

Allow your awareness to come right back into the middle of yourself, in your deeper breathing, present in this moment.

This moment of your experience is a sacrament of God's presence.

What is it like to allow that, to be open to that possibility in yourself? Does this allow your suffering to be felt more keenly? Now do one simple thing: look out the window, or look at a book, or have a sip of coffee *without* losing that awareness of being in this moment, but now with that added activity.

We can experiment with this in ordinary life. How far can we engage life with this awareness? Where is it lost? Is it easy or hard to take it up again?

Julian's Present Moment in Jesus

If you have an image of Jesus in his suffering, practise the awareness of being in this present moment, as described above, and then look at this image of Jesus in his Passion. Stay with the image.

What do you feel?
What thoughts emerge?
What would you say to him? What might he say to you?

As Julian invites us to live within the belief that we are experiencing God constantly, try taking moments of life, perhaps
using the meditation above, to experiment with being open to
life in this way.

6

God in a Point

Julian's Showing 3 seems at first glance to be completely different from Showing 2. Jesus is not mentioned anywhere in this
Showing, let alone his suffering or death. Julian seems to have
moved in this Showing into an entirely different spiritual universe. We will discover, however, that as we engage with
Showing 3, and live within the vision it unfolds, we arrive at
nearly the same spiritual practice as already seen in Showing 2:
a sustained, poised openness to this moment as the place where
God, in Jesus, already is.

God in a Point

Showing 3 begins with Julian seeing, as she says, 'God in a
point':

> And after this [Julian says] I saw God in a point – that is to
> say, in my understanding – and by seeing this I saw that he is in
> everything. (BW, LT 11)

In seeing God in everything, Julian has returned to something
like the 'hazelnut' vision in the first Showing, in which she saw
divine love as the ground of creation. In this third Showing,
not only does she see God as the ground of all being, and in all
things, but even, mysteriously, as the agent of all that is done.

I looked attentively, seeing and recognizing in that vision that
[God] *does everything that is done.* I marvelled at that sight
with quiet awe ... (BW, LT 11, emphasis mine)

Such a vision of God in all things, and providentially doing all
that is done, is not without difficulty. If God is in all things, and
the doer of all that is done, what then is sin, Julian asks, and
what is evil, and can we even affirm the human judgement of
good and bad, virtue and vice?

[I] thought, 'What is sin?' For I saw truly that God does
everything, however small it may be. And I saw truly that
nothing is done by chance or accident but everything by God's
prescient wisdom. (BW, LT 11)

Such questions about the reality of sin, within a vision of God
in all and doing all, and about the necessity of human discern-
ment between good and evil, are critical questions, and they will
follow Julian through several more chapters of the *Revelations*
until they are finally addressed in Showing 13.

At this early point in the *Revelations*, however, Julian is not
ready to face such questions. While she observes a stark difference in how we judge things – some as good, some bad, some
trivial, some important – and how God judges them, she is swept
along by the force of the mystical experience itself, not only seeing God in all things, doing all that is done, but experiencing
God's *satisfaction and joy* with all things just as they are.

I saw most certainly that [God] never changes his purpose in
any kind of thing, nor ever shall, eternally ... for [God] made
everything in fullness of goodness; and therefore the blessed
Trinity is always completely satisfied with all his works. And
he showed all this most blessedly with this meaning, 'See, I am
God. See, I am in everything. See, I do everything. See, I never
lift my hands from my works, nor ever shall, without end.
See, I guide everything to the end to which I ordained it from
without beginning by the same power, wisdom, and love with
which I made it. How should anything be amiss?' (BW, LT 11)

Julian admits that this last question – How should anything be amiss? – was a test for her. For Julian, as for all of us, a great many things are very much amiss! But at this point Julian does not engage the tension between her sense of wrongness in the world and God's unconstrained affirmation of all. Rather, she simply lets all her concern go to surrender herself to the flow of God's joy:

> Thus powerfully, wisely, and lovingly was the soul tested in this vision. Then I saw truly that I must give my assent with great reverence, rejoicing in God. (BW, LT 11)

Two Eckharts and the Joy of Being

Eckhart Tolle, the hugely popular spiritual writer and mystic from the start of the twenty-first century, wrote about the experience of the joy of Being in itself in his book *The Power of Now*. For Tolle, this joy in being could be known and surrendered to, in the cessation of thinking and judging, opening our sheer attentive presence to the reality of the Now. This echoed a similar kind of spirituality that emerged in late medieval times, such as in Meister Eckhart, who lived a century before Julian and is known for his mysticism of detachment and surrender to God in the wordless awareness of Uncreated Being. Eckhart Tolle, Meister Eckhart and Julian have widely diverging theologies, but here is something similar happening in terms of the raw spiritual experience of God.

A Spiritual Experiment?

But what are we to make of Julian's original experience in Showing 3 – seeing God in a point, in all things, doing all that is done, and satisfied with each moment of creation, so that nothing could be considered amiss? Unlike Julian, most of us are not having this mystical experience. How can we make this real for ourselves, even for the least mystical among us? How are we to make this kind of vision our own?

Showing 2 encouraged us to make a spiritual experiment – taking on as an assumption that we are already experiencing God, and seeing what life is like when approached in this way. Similarly, Showing 3 encourages another spiritual experiment, which centres on the marked difference that Julian saw between human ways of judging and God's apparent satisfaction with all that is. Julian writes:

> [A] man regards some deeds as well done and some deeds as evil, but our Lord does not regard them so; for as everything that exists in nature is of God's making, so everything that is done is an aspect of God's doing. For it is easy to understand that the best deed is well done; and the least deed is done as well as the best and the most exalted; and all in the manner and order that our Lord has ordained from without beginning, for there is no doer but he. (BW, LT 11)

What Julian actually *does* with this in Showing 3 is to surrender entirely the human way of judging – in which some things are very much amiss – to experience God's way of judging, in which nothing is amiss. This was possible for Julian because she was being carried along by the power of mystical experience: she was not thinking about how God relates to the world, she was experiencing a flow of joy and satisfaction that seemed to penetrate all things.

Most of us are not mystics, or at least not having this kind of experience, so we can't join Julian directly in her experience in Showing 3; but what we can do is to experiment with what it is like to release our faculty of judging, our instinctive habit of sorting every experience into good or bad. I will call this experiment that of 'suspending our faculty of judging' because this captures well the sense, *not* of trying to work ourselves up to a mystical fervour, *nor* of trying to work out how everything could be filled with God, but more simply of suspending the habit of judging, and seeing what life feels like when we do this.

The best way to do this is in a meditation that explores what happens when we drop our habitual judging with something in life that has caused us irritation, an irritation we can feel but which does not overwhelm us.

A Guided Meditation: The Suspension of Judgement and the Mystery of Jesus

For the meditation, or spiritual experiment, we might first want to settle ourselves in a comfortable place where we'll have 10 or 20 minutes to ourselves.

We can then call to mind something from our lives that has been very much *amiss*, some wrong we have suffered or some unjust pain endured, something we instinctively condemn. This needs to be important enough to elicit some reaction in us, but not so overwhelmingly horrible as to block our imaginative process.

As we call this moderately painful thing to mind, we can notice the energy of our negative judgement pushing against this 'bad thing'. We naturally want to hold this bad thing at arm's length.

As we sit with this experience we can notice, however, that the force of our negative judgement, condemning this 'bad thing', does not in fact get rid of it! This is key. In a strange way, our condemning of something keeps us locked into it. We are left there, holding it at arm's length, trying to make it go away, but it still pushes back on us. It still asserts its reality. As long as we are condemning it, saying it should not be there, it presents itself all the more strongly. It's as if we are saying that something that does exist should not exist (which might be true), but it nonetheless does exist, and its very reality presses all the more strongly on us as we condemn it.

Normally, the only way out of this locked-in conflict with what causes us pain is just to let the condemned reality fall into the background of our awareness and direct our attention to something else.

What happens, however, if instead of just forgetting about the painful thing, we allow it to be there in all its reality, and also allow the stiff arm of our condemnation of it to fall away? We stop trying to hold it at arm's length. This is not the same as actively *wanting* it to be there, or approving it. We are not saying yes to it; we are only suspending our judgement about it.

This can be a very special moment.

The first thing that we can notice is some fear in ourselves. It is scary to let go of our condemnation.

However, we can also feel that, in no longer attempting to push the 'bad thing' away from ourselves, two things happen.

First, how we feel is not so locked into this previously condemned reality. The condemned reality is still there, but we are not determined by it. We can begin to see or feel around it as long as we are not trying to push it away.

Second, as we allow the 'condemned thing' to be there without judgement, we can also begin to feel all the hurt of it, the suffering in it, more sensitively.

The result of this little experiment is that we can safely be more in touch with the reality of what we formerly insisted on condemning, without being overwhelmed by it. We may even begin to feel some tenderness for ourselves and others and for the hurt that is there. We become in this way more vulnerable to this 'bad thing' when we suspend our judging faculty, but also more free from it. We can courageously and creatively choose to do something about it. We can also offer it to God.

Jesus was a scandal because he did not condemn 'bad' people. He forgave his friends who abandoned and betrayed him and even those who tortured and killed him. What we attain in this meditation/spiritual experiment, however, is not quite forgiveness – that might come later. Rather, we reach a new capacity to offer the condemned situation up to God, for God's healing, for God's care, for God's forgiveness. In other words, we reach the possibility of real prayer and real intercession about this hurt reality. We have accepted its reality (not pretending it is good), and so we can begin to be part of its healing by offering it to God who can take care of it.

This is, in short, the practice of intercession, and it shares in something we see in Jesus on the cross: not condemning the world, but vulnerable to the world and offering the world up to

God. Where both Showing 2 and Showing 3 take us, in spite of their radically different content, is to a practice of offering our world, our daily experience, this moment now, up to God. This is such a humble thing! It is not taking responsibility for the moment. Still less is it playing theological mind games with ourselves to make what seems bad really good in God. It is a humble practice of offering what is right before us up to God. This is a living way of prayer, and the more we do it, the more we find that it is a creative way of engaging with life as itself a response to God, not only in the big picture, but in the small things, in this moment right in front of us.

Questions for Reflection and Discussion

1 Have you attempted the guided reflection offered in this chapter? What was this like? Why or why not did you find this helpful?

2 Can you imagine attempting this kind of spiritual experiment as a way of intercession, for instance when you are asked to pray for someone stuck in an apparently intractable and difficult situation?

3 Can you imagine doing this experiment *now*, with whatever is before you, being open to this, getting to know what is happening, inside and outside you, and offering this to God's care?

4 Have you had unitive experiences like the one Julian describes in this Showing, in which all seems blessed and rejoiced in? Or moments like this, or hints of this? If so, how have you squared this with the experience of so much wrongness and hurt in the rest of life?

7

A Sequence of Minor Showings

Showings 4, 5 and 6 are minor Showings which, though brief, broaden our sense of Julian's religious world, adding theological meaning and devotional depth. Showing 4 reveals the power of Julian's religious imagination, Showing 5 is more theological about the meaning of Jesus' Passion, and in Showing 6, Julian experiences again something of God's homely joy. In Showing 7, she shares the volatility in her spiritual state, which prepares Julian, and us her readers, for the emotional challenge of Showing 8.

Showing 4: A Healing Flow of Blood

Julian returns to her vision of the suffering Jesus, particularly his bleeding, in Showing 4.

> And after this I saw, as I watched, the body bleeding profusely in weals from the scourging ... the hot blood ran out so abundantly that neither skin nor wound was to be seen, but it seemed as if it were all blood ... the bleeding continued for a while, so that it could be observed with deliberation. And it was so abundant to my way of seeing that it seemed to me that if it had been the real thing in nature [that is, not a mystical vision] ... it would have saturated the bed with blood and overflowed all around ... it is most abundant as it is most precious, and that is so by virtue of his blessed Godhead. (BW, LT 12)

What fascinates Julian is the sheer *abundance* of the blood. Reversing the usual economy of what is most precious being most rare, this blood is 'most abundant as it is most precious'. Divine love gives freely and most abundantly precisely what is most needful. This sight of Jesus' blood becomes, in her imagination, a cosmic vision: the blood of Jesus washing over the whole earth and into hell to liberate those condemned there.

> The beloved blood of our Lord Jesus Christ is as truly most precious as it is truly abundant. Behold and see! The precious plenty of his beloved blood descended down into hell and broke their bonds and delivered all those who were there who belonged to the court of heaven. The precious plenty of his beloved blood overflows the whole earth and is ready to wash from sin all who are, have been, and shall be of good will. (BW, LT 12)

The flood of blood even returns up into the heavens where it is part of God's rejoicing.

> The precious plenty of his beloved blood ascended up into heaven ... And it flows through all heaven for ever more, rejoicing ... (BW, LT 12)

This flow of blood is caused by suffering, and yet the whole point of the Showing is to induce not guilt (at how much we have made Jesus suffer), but joy and gratitude for the flowing of Jesus' life to us, healing and redeeming. The unqualified nature of this healing flow of blood, from the totality of Jesus' self-gift, is important. It flows over all things, all creation, and even into hell, so that nothing is left untouched by this offering in love of cleansing and liberation. Nothing in creation is untouched by this healing flow, and nothing of God is held back.

Showing 5: The Fiend Overcome

Following Showing 4, Showing 5 begins with God allowing Julian time to contemplate all that she has seen of Jesus. Then God speaks words to her that summarize and give meaning to all that she has experienced.

> And afterwards, before God revealed any words, he allowed me to contemplate him for a suitable time, and all that I had seen, and all the significance in it, as far as the simplicity of my soul could take it in. Then he ... formed in my soul these words: 'In this way the devil is overcome.' Our Lord said these words referring to his blessed Passion, as he had shown it before. (BW, LT 13)

There is something tender and caring in God's first allowing Julian time to contemplate, to integrate, to understand what she has seen. Likewise, our faith needs time to develop. It does not happen quickly with assent to a certain belief or a simple desire to trust in God, but matures into deep believing and a true opening of self in trust through prolonged rumination on images and words that speak of God's love for us.

Theologically, in this Showing we are presented with the ringing affirmation that Jesus' Passion is what overcomes all evil, all destructiveness, all that has enslaved and disfigured our humanity. God is saying to Julian, and Julian to us, that what ultimately undoes the power of fear, anger and division in our lives, what heals the wounds we have suffered, what teaches us a less violent and less selfish way of being, is the Word of God's closeness and love spoken in Jesus' suffering and death. Contact between this word of love and our lives is what overcomes all evil; it is what heals and redeems.

In a wonderfully human moment, Julian laughs as she sees God turn all the devil's apparently tragic and unredeemable work into our glory and future happiness. The devil is powerless to stop God from using all that the devil does for God's greater glory.

I also saw our Lord scorn his malice and discount [the devil's] powerlessness, and he wants us to do the same. At the sight of this I laughed heartily, and that made those who were around me to laugh, and their laughter was a pleasure to me. In my thoughts I wished that all my fellow Christians had seen what I saw, and then they would all have laughed with me. (BW, LT 13)

Showing 6: A Marvellous Melody of Love

In Showing 6, the last of these three Showings, Julian is thanked by God for her service and suffering, and she is shown some of the joy of heaven where we are thanked by God.

After this our good Lord said, 'I thank you for your service and your suffering, and especially in your youth.' And with this my understanding was lifted up into heaven, where I saw our Lord as a lord in his own house, who has called all his beloved servants and friends to a splendid feast. (BW, LT 14)

Returning to the theme of homeliness, Julian sees God not royally enthroned even in heaven, but serving and spreading joy around his guests:

I saw the Lord take no seat in his own house, but I saw him reign royally in his house, and he filled it full of joy and delight, himself eternally gladdening and comforting his beloved friends most friendlily and most courteously, with marvellous melody of endless love in his own fair, blessed face, which glorious face of the Godhead fills heavens full of joy and bliss. (BW, LT 14)

Julian goes on to reflect on different aspects of our joy in heaven, but she focuses particularly on God's gratitude to us, with which she began the Showing. And this perhaps can be an encouragement to us: that because of our faithful cooperation with God's working in how we are with ourselves and in our world, God is grateful to us as to fellow workers and fellow sufferers.

Showing 7: Julian returns to herself

In Showing 7, Julian begins to come back to herself. Instead of receiving more spiritual insights and impressions, in this Showing Julian begins to feel instead her internal response to all that has come before. With extreme volatility, Julian swings between divine consolation and human desolation. It's as though the only way she can hold on to both herself in her suffering and her experience of God is to swing rapidly between the two. Julian describes this experience with remarkable candour:

> [God] revealed a supreme spiritual delight in my soul. In this delight I was filled full of everlasting certainty, powerfully sustained, without any fear to pain me. This feeling was so joyful and so spiritual that I was wholly at peace, at ease, and at rest, so that there was nothing on earth that could have distressed me.
>
> This only lasted a while, and my mood turned right round and I was left to myself, feeling depressed, weary of my life and disgusted with myself, so that I could hardly have the patience to go on living. (BW, LT 15)

But then the joy comes back:

> And immediately after this our blessed Lord again gave me comfort and rest in my soul, with pleasure and certainty so blissful and so powerful that no fear, no sorrow, no pain bodily nor spiritual that one might suffer could have troubled me. And then I felt this pain again ... and then the joy and the delight ... (BW, LT 15)

Julian says that she alternates between these two extremes not once or twice, but 'about twenty times'! As these mood shifts happened so rapidly and were so extreme, Julian is also aware that she did nothing to cause or deserve either the good or bad moods. She concludes that the moods were part of God's loving care for her: sometimes consoling her, but sometimes leaving her to experience directly her own suffering, as if in God's absence.

In either situation, Julian sees that she is protected by the same love.

> This vision was shown me to teach me – as I understand it – that it is helpful for some souls to feel in this way: sometimes to be comforted, and sometimes to feel failure and be left to themselves. God wants us to know that he keeps us equally safe in sorrow and in joy. And for the benefit of his soul a [person] is sometimes left to himself, although sin is not always the cause. (BW, LT 15)

Almost more than any other, this particular Showing has proved itself of immense practical value to people attempting to live a life of faith. We are consoled that Julian herself could feel such oscillation and such extremity, and that neither extremity is more about love or being close to God, or our sinfulness or virtue. Rather, the experience of extremes, even those of spiritual desolation, can be part of God's care for us in love. We might surmise from this that God's love does not mean an escape from the hurt and suffering of our lives, but rather support to face these more squarely so that they might be brought consciously into contact with God's Word in Jesus, and made available for healing. God leaves us to ourselves so that we can know ourselves, but God also consoles and cares for us as he does so.

Conclusion: Prepared for the Challenge of Showing 8

We have already travelled far with Julian. Through these initial seven Showings we have seen an understanding of faith emerge as an openness to a God of loving compassion who is present in every experience, and who asks us to be open to ourselves as we experience life. As we welcome God, we must also welcome ourselves and our experience, because this is where God has already chosen to be – this is arguably the basic meaning of Jesus' incarnation and our faith in Jesus. But this threefold opening in tenderness and compassion (to God, ourselves and our world), as Showing 7 reveals, is not always an easy process because of the disparity of what we are opening to and the extremity of feelings. In Showing 8, Julian will confront directly the challenge of this kind of compassionate and faithful openness that Jesus inspired in her.

Questions for Reflection and Discussion

1   Recall the Showings we have experienced so far:
    i   Jesus in homely love showing us his suffering but also the bliss of God.
    ii   God present but hidden in all our experience, even our suffering.
    iii God blissfully affirming all things.
    iv   God's blood cleansing all of creation.
    v   Jesus' death overcoming the devil.
    vi   God thanking us for our service in faith.
    vii Julian's fluctuation between suffering and joy, but held always in one love.
    Take some time to reflect on these in turn. What do you remember most? Which seems most important to you?
2   We have touched briefly on some spiritual practices, like contemplative prayer, or living more in the present moment as the moment of God's presence, or suspending our judging faculty to bring the world before God in intercession. We have also dwelt on devotion to the person of Jesus in his Passion as God's healing word of love. Do any of these practices speak most to you? How could you follow up your interest?
3   Thus far in this book, faith is emerging as something that includes objective belief and invites subjective trust. For example, we believe that God is love, and we are invited to place our trust in that love. It's also becoming clear that such faith is not a one-off event, a sudden decision to believe something or a moment of self-surrender. Rather, it's a life-long process in which all that is afraid and perhaps hostile to

love is brought into contact with God for healing – not only within ourselves, but in our relationships and in our world. A life of faith is thus a commitment to remain open to both our reality and God's reality, and to be a place where these two can meet. Can this be seen as a valid purpose in life as a whole? Is this big enough to include all your aspirations and commitments?

8

Who Is My Heaven?

Introduction: A Graphic Journey into Jesus' Death

In Showing 8, which spans Chapters 16–21, Julian returns to her experience of Jesus' Passion, which she first encountered in Showing 1 and elaborated in Showings 2, 4 and 5. As a graphic meditation on Jesus' physical sufferings, this is one of the most difficult Showings in all the *Revelations*. It is also one of the most meaningful, because in it Julian's spirituality, as grounded in compassion and acceptance, is tested directly in a spiritual crisis.

Building gradually to the point of this test, the Showing begins with Julian seeing the suffering of Jesus, mainly in the discolouration of his face.

> After this Christ showed part of his Passion, close to his death. I saw his dear face as it was dry and bloodless with the pallor of death; and then more deathly pale, in anguish, and then turning blue as death advanced, and afterwards a darker blue as death took more hold on his flesh. For his Passion was revealed to me most distinctly in his blessed face, and especially in his lips. There I saw these four colours, which before had appeared fresh and ruddy, full of life and lovely to see. This was a grievous change, to see this deep dying, and also, as it seemed to me, the nose shrivelled and dried up, and the dear body was brown and black ... (BW, LT 16)

This graphic sight of Jesus' suffering extends for another chapter and a half. Julian sees, for instance, the crown of thorns now ringed with flesh and dried blood:

I saw that the dear skin and the tender flesh, with the hair and the blood, was all lifted and loosened away from the bone by the thorns with which it had been slashed in many places, like a sagging cloth ... (BW, LT 17)

And she feels the dryness, coldness and thirst of Christ as he dies.

[I]t seemed to me that there was a dry, keen wind and terribly cold; and it was revealed that when all the precious blood that could bleed from the dear body had bled from it, there still remained some moisture in Christ's dear flesh. Loss of blood and pain drying him inside, and the blowing of the wind and cold coming from outside, met together in the dear body of Christ. (BW, LT 16)

Julian notes that there is a spiritual meaning to Jesus' physical thirst from this drying:

And in this drying there came to my mind Christ's words: 'I thirst.' For I saw in Christ a double thirst: one bodily, the other spiritual (of which I shall speak in the thirty-first chapter). For in these words the bodily thirst was revealed, and I shall say later what was revealed concerning the spiritual thirst. (BW, LT 17)

In gazing on the discoloured and desiccated body of Jesus, Julian feels she is seeing a body that is dying of love for us, a thirsting need unto death to draw us into himself.

The Mystery of Compassion: Jesus' Bodily Experience is Julian's Bodily Experience

What are we then to make of this graphic vision of Christ's suffering? We can certainly regard this as an interesting account of a fourteenth-century religious experience, no doubt informed by the devotional culture of her time, but it is hard to see its bearing on us.

The first clue that Julian's experience in Showing 8 will have meaning for us is found in her sudden declaration that she was not merely witnessing Jesus' suffering as a spectator but was experiencing his thirst, cold and general pain, directly in her own body.

> The revelation of Christ's pains filled me full of pain, for I was well aware that he only suffered once, but he wanted to show it to me *and fill me with the recollection of it*, as I had earlier wished. And in all this time that Christ was present to me, I felt no pain except for Christ's pains. (BW, LT 17, emphasis mine)

It is as if Jesus' bodily experience becomes Julian's bodily self-experience; how he felt in his body is how she felt in hers.

This should give us pause. There is perhaps nothing more rudimentary in our experience of being a self, an individual, than the feeling each of us has of being this particular body here. But something happens in Showing 8, such that this most basic boundary between Jesus and Julian becomes permeable, and then dissolves, so that the two self-experiences flow in and out of each other, Jesus into Julian and Julian into Jesus.

Julian's Withdrawal from Compassion

For Julian, this experience of Jesus became too much to bear and she pulls back from it:

> I thought to myself, 'I little knew what pain it was that I asked for', and like a wretch I regretted it, thinking, 'If I had known what it would be like, I would have been reluctant to pray for it', for it seemed to me that my pains exceeded bodily death. (BW, LT 17)

In regretting that she had asked to be so intimate with Jesus, Julian was, in effect, already pulling back from the experience of Christ, putting distance, if not a wall, between her experience and his. This is no light thing: it goes against Julian's most basic desire to be a friend of Jesus by compassionately sharing his experience with him, which was from the beginning the most elemental and instinctive aspect of Julian's spirituality and faith. Julian calls herself a 'wretch' for having pulled back from Jesus.

Divine and Creaturely Compassion Explored

Following this confession, the next chapter is an *intellectual discourse* on the mystery of compassion. It's as if Julian, instead of experiencing compassion, chooses instead to reflect on it from a distance.

Such reflection is, however, not without significant insight. To begin with, Julian reverses the traditional idea that Jesus in his Passion is suffering all human trauma. This is true, as she says elsewhere (LT 20), but so is the opposite: that all our suffering, and even all suffering in creation itself, is our participation in Jesus' Passion.

> Here I saw a great affinity between Christ and us ... for when he was in pain, we were in pain. And all creatures capable of suffering pain suffered with him ... The firmament and the earth failed out of sorrow in their very nature at the moment of Christ's death ... So was our Lord Jesus set at nought for us, and we all remain in this way as if set at nought with him, and shall do until we come to his bliss, as I shall say later. (BW, LT 18)

We are set at nought with him in the daily sufferings of life, just as he is set at nought for us, in taking on our pain and violence and sin out of love. And even though his Passion is now over, Julian affirms that Jesus suffers with us still:

> For as long as he was liable to suffer, he suffered for us and sorrowed for us; and now he is risen again and no longer liable to suffering, he still suffers with us. (BW, LT 20)

... and all our suffering is suffering with him:

I understood that we are now – in our Lord's intention – dying on his cross with him in our pain and our sufferings. (BW, LT 21)

This flow of our experience into Jesus, and his Passion into us, as a mystery of compassion, is unqualified, unconstrained and unavoidable. Julian invites us to see Jesus' suffering as our own, and ours as his, as a fundamental reality in our creation. This theological sense of a universe open in compassion, tied irrevocably into the person of Jesus and suffering in resonance with him, undergirds the devotional and therapeutic experience that we might have of encountering our own Passions as we gaze on Jesus in his Passion. This is something we have seen earlier: being in touch with Jesus' hurt and dying body with tenderness for him, openness and compassion, is an indirect way of also being in touch with our hurt bodies and souls. Jesus in his hurt body holds the suffering of our lives and our world, contains it, gives it a home in himself, and yet he still wants to be open in love to us.

Who Shall Our Heaven Be?

Julian is not allowed, however, to reflect at a distance on the mystery of compassion for too long. Soon, the crisis that began with her initial regret that she was suffering with Jesus comes to a head, and Julian faces a question that tests the foundation of her entire spirituality. Does she want in fact to be open to Jesus, and thus to her own suffering and the hardship of human reality and the world as it is? Does she want such compassion and acceptance to be the hallmark of her spirituality and how she enacts her faithfulness to God? Or does she want a spirituality that will allow her to transcend human vulnerability, either in Jesus or herself: a transcendental escape from suffering earth to heaven?[2] Does she want compassion that opens up simultan-

---

2 I owe this insight in the first instance to Julia Gatta, who wrote about this question as a temptation to a transcendental spirituality in her book *Three Spiritual Directors for Our Time*, Cambridge, MA: Cowley Publications, 1986, p. 72.

eously to self, other and God, or does she want escape into a pure experience of God alone?

This question comes to Julian explicitly in her inner dialogue. As she tells us:

> At this time I wanted to look up from the cross [the sight of which she feels is the source of her suffering] and I did not dare ...
>
> Then I thought my reason suggested to me, as if there had been said to me in a friendly way, 'Look up to heaven to his Father.' And then I saw clearly, with the faith that I felt, that there was nothing between the cross and heaven which could have distressed me. Either I must look up or else reply. (BW, LT 19)

'Look up to heaven to his Father!' Julian can either stay with Jesus in compassion, or she can look up to God the Father. Julian's answer is a resounding choice to stay open to Jesus in his suffering, and thus open to herself.

> I answered inwardly with all my soul's strength and said, 'No, I cannot, for you are my heaven.' I said this because I did not want to look up; for I would rather have remained in that pain until Judgement Day than come to heaven in any other way than by him ... So I was taught to choose Jesus for my heaven, whom I saw only in pain at that time. (BW, LT 19)

Julian chooses Jesus for her heaven. This is also a choice to stay with herself, and to stay open to the reality of this world as her enacted faithfulness to God, because this God in Jesus has already chosen to be open in compassion to all of Julian's reality and all the reality of the world. If we have a block in any of these areas – if we can't bear to face some part of ourselves, for instance, or some part of the world – it will throw up a block in the other areas as well. Compassion is how Julian invites us to enact our faith in God's love in Jesus, to make him our heaven in suffering and in joy, and this compassion is a threefold flower that opens at once in tenderness to self, and others, and God.

Compassion or Relief?

Applying this to ourselves, we can ask of our prayer, our going to church, our rumination on sacred texts and gazing on holy images, our enjoyment of liturgy and music: is all this meant to give us a 'nice religious or spiritual experience' off to the side of the rest of life? If we practise contemplative prayer, meditation and mindfulness, is this meant merely to give us relief from life, stepping aside from ourselves into a pleasing, temporary calm? Does our service to the poor, and our seeking after social justice and political equity, spring merely from a need to add a dimension of goodness to our lives, something we can feel positive about? Whatever our spirituality is, and whatever our practice of faith, Julian's Showing 8 puts before us a fundamental question: are we doing this in response to God's compassion, opening ourselves ever more to ourselves and our world, or are we doing this merely to add something 'nice' to our lives, or as a relief and escape from life?

Questions for Reflection and Discussion

1 Can you remember and describe the time when you chose to be Christian, chose to follow Christ? Perhaps this was a dramatic moment of being 'born again', or perhaps it was something that gradually dawned on you. What was it that drew you to Jesus or Christianity? Is the person of Jesus still at the centre of your faith, or has this shifted to something else?

2 Compassion and tenderness, to self, world, and God in Jesus, is how Julian enacts her faith and her love. Do you see compassion as being this primary, this central, or is there some other value, such as honesty or clarity, that seems more fundamental?

3 Some of our spiritual practices are more like a vacation from normal life, others are more 'additive', in adding a good experience, and some are 'transformative' because

in them we open some aspect of ourselves or our world to God's compassionate care. Are there parts of your religious and/or spiritual practice that are more like an escape from life, times when you take a break? Are there parts of your religious and spiritual practice that add positive or meaningful experiences on to the rest of your life? Are there aspects of your life where you are able to be open to *more* of yourself and to more of others in compassion, such that you can then offer these to God? Does prayer do this for you, does loving relationship, does meditation, or a walk in the woods, or going to church?

9

Are You Well Satisfied?

Introduction: A Mystic of Compassion, a Mystic of the Ordinary

Showing 8 was the climactic moment in Julian's experience of the Passion of Jesus, and as such it was the moment in which the very nature of her faith in God and her spirituality, as based in compassion, was proved beyond doubt. Julian's spirituality is not one of escape, or relief, but of ever-increasing openness in loving compassion to self, world and God.

This kind of faith makes, on reflection, a paradox for readers of Julian. On the one hand, Julian had supernatural, mystical experiences of God. On the other hand, the kind of God revealed in the *Revelations* is one who is with us in our sheer ordinariness and vulnerability of being human. This is a God who is, in a way, more surrendered to being just human than we ourselves are, and who invites us to join Godself there. Julian is a mystic of the ordinary because she is a mystic of divine compassion, and her mystical experiences thus all serve to orientate us towards the ordinary experience of daily life as the place where God is, and is at work.

A Transformation into Joy

For her part, once Julian makes her surrender to Jesus as her heaven, it's as though she passes through a threshold from suffering into an experience of God's delight in loving us. Julian describes the exact moment of this transformation:

I watched [the suffering Jesus] with all my might for the moment of his passing away and expected to see the body quite dead, but I did not see him so. And just at the very moment when, to all appearances, it seemed to me that life could last no longer and there must be a revelation of his end, suddenly, as I was looking at the same cross, his blessed countenance changed. The change in his blessed expression changed mine, and I was as glad and happy as it is possible to be. Then our Lord brought to mind the happy thought, 'Is there any point now to your pain or your sorrow?' And I was very happy. (BW, LT 21)

Christ's face changes and, with that, Julian's inner reality changes as well. Never again in the *Revelations* will Julian contemplate the suffering body of Jesus in his Passion. Here all is transformed. Following this point, a series of four brief Showings follows, Showings 9 to 12, all characterized by heavenly joy.

Are You Well Satisfied?

In Showing 9, God engages Julian in a lively conversation, probing to see if she can be satisfied with God's way of responding in love to our human situation as seen in the *Revelations* thus far. Jesus asks Julian, 'Are you well pleased that I suffered for you?' Julian responds:

'Yes, good Lord, thank you. Yes, good Lord, blessed may you be.' Then Jesus, our kind Lord, said, 'If you are pleased, then I am pleased. It is a joy, a bliss, an endless delight to me that I ever suffered my Passion for you; and if I could suffer more, I would suffer more.' (BW, LT 22)

The Middle English phrase translated above as 'well pleased' is 'well apaid'. This is commonly translated as 'well satisfied' (JJS, LT 22; see also BW, LT 22). Jesus is thus asking Julian if she can be *well satisfied* by his Passion, and the use of this phrase is key because 'satisfaction', being 'well apaid', was a key theological term in medieval England.

In the standard theology of Julian's time, still popular in our own, the Passion of Jesus is understood as 'satisfying' God, not us. In this view, Jesus' suffering and death satisfies God, either by slaking God's wrath at our wrongdoing, or in satisfying God's regretful need to enforce divine justice on a sinful humanity. In this traditional view, Jesus' Passion *satisfies* God; it makes it possible for God to let us, as it were, into heaven. We become acceptable to God through Jesus' self-offering.

Julian's visionary experience of God in the *Revelations* inverts this entire story.

In Julian's world view, the wrathfulness, or the sense of justice, that need to be satisfied, are not in God, but in us. This is absolutely critical. Already Julian has encountered a God who loves us unconditionally. Now this God turns to Julian and asks her if she can be 'satisfied' with God because of the suffering and death of Jesus, if this is enough for her. This hints at later developments in the *Revelations*, explored in chapter 12 of this book, in which Julian will clearly say that what stops us from being one with God is not God's wrath, but our wrath, not God's sense of justice, but our offended sense of justice at how the world is, at how our lives have been. Jesus presents his Passion (which is to say his choice to remain lovingly open to all of Julian and all of the world), asking her if this is enough to slake her wrath and offended sense of justice – if she can, in other words, accept and be at peace with herself, her life and the world, and with God who, as the creator, is responsible for all of this.

Can we be satisfied with this way of God's loving, God's coming in Jesus in compassion, and God's working secretly in the Holy Spirit to make us more loving and peaceful, as this is revealed in Julian's experience and writings?

A New Heaven and a New Earth?

Julian sharpens such questions by comparing two different ways in which one can imagine God working to make us 'satisfied' with the way things are. God, Julian realizes, could have satisfied us by choosing to remake creation more to our liking. Alternatively, God could choose to join us in our human condition exactly as it is and to make it the medium through which love is given.

> [I]n these words – 'If I could suffer more, I would suffer more' – I truly saw that he was willing to die just as often as he was able to die, and love would never let him rest until he had done it ... For if he said that, for love of me, he would make new heavens and a new earth, that would only be small in comparison, for he could do this every day if he wished, without any effort. (BW, LT 22)

God could make new heavens and a new earth; but God, as Julian experienced the divine, chose a different way, one that for Julian seemed more noble and more self-giving.

> But to die for love of me so often that the number passes human understanding, that is the noblest offer that our Lord God could make to man's soul, as I see it. This, then, is his meaning, 'How could it then be that I should not do all I could for love of you? To do so does not grieve me, since I would die so often for love of you, without regard to my cruel pains.' (BW, LT 22)

Listening to Our Dissatisfaction and Our Wrath

It is natural for us to grieve at how our world is, at how life has been for us. It is understandable to feel that we cannot give life the unqualified 'Yes!' to which God invites us, or to feel that divine compassion, even in its fullest sense, could never make everything well for us.

Most of us feel, in fact, wrathful or bitter about parts of ourselves, our lives or the way the world is. We worry that allowing ourselves to be satisfied with the way things are would be to become complicit in the evils and horrors we find in our world. In this way, our protest against the way things are serves to protect our basic dignity as human beings, and the dignity of the world: it should not be this way, that people suffer like this, and that we have suffered as we have. To be satisfied with the way things are seems either callous or spineless, unable to stand up for and protect the dignity of our own humanity.

What Julian's Showing 9 asks of us is this: what is the better way to personal healing, what is the better spring for creative action for the betterment of our world, what better protects our inviolate sense of the dignity of every human being? Is it our wrath, our protest, our dissatisfaction? Or is it the revelation of Jesus' loving closeness to each human being, his embrace of the most horrible moments of human history and personal experience? In the first instance, we are protected by striking out against an apparent wrong. In the second instance, we are in touch with an energy of love and care that touches our life and those of others.

The wager we are being invited to consider by Julian's ninth Showing is that allowing Jesus to be our heaven – that is, the compassionate presence of God in every human being and every human experience – is in fact better than wrath as a way of pro-tecting our fundamental dignity as human beings, a better spring for creative action to right the injustice of the world, a better way to personal healing and transformation.

Our dissatisfaction and our wrath are still important: they are like the inflammation around wounds in our souls and societies. Inflammation serves to alarm and protect. There is perhaps no safer way to let go of such wrath that sounds the alarm and provides immediate protection than in the assurance of a divine love that cares infinitely for all of us, that has already joined us in our hurt and defacement, and that invites us now to cooperate in God's healing of ourselves and the world.

Questions for Reflection and Discussion

1 Is Jesus' Passion enough for me personally? Can I identify areas of my life where I feel grieved, resentful or angry at what happened to me, or at what I myself did? Recognizing that such past situations are now unchangeable, does it help

to imagine Jesus dying with me in them, and with others in that situation? Do I recover any dignity from Jesus' acceptance?

2 In *The Brothers Karamazov* by Dostoevsky (Book 5, Ch. 4), a character refuses faith on the grounds of the infinite injustice of the suffering of one human child. Does Julian's Showing 9 offer an adequate response to this? Is it enough to say, 'Yes, this is a horrible reality and a horrible injustice, but God suffers the injustice too and promises a healing and a joyous outcome in the end?' Does this sense of divine suffering in every human suffering make you more likely to seek to address such suffering?

3 C. S. Lewis wrote that, in the twentieth century, God is in the dock, in the sense that human beings are accusing God of fundamental injustice in how God has allowed the world to be. The ancient arguments about humanity *deserving* suffering from Original Sin no longer seem tenable or acceptable; God needs to answer for the wrongs we encounter in life. Do we, as judge and jury and prosecutor with God in the dock, continue to press charges against God, or does the image of the suffering Jesus, the 'infinitely gentle, infinitely suffering thing', to borrow T. S. Eliot's phrase, draw out the sting of our anger and our accusation against God? Can we be satisfied?

10

A Cloven Heart, Mary in Bliss, the Glory of God

Showings 10, 11 and 12 are brief and intense Showings in which Julian experiences different aspects of the joy of heaven.

Showing 10: A Place for All of Humanity to Abide

Julian enjoys, in Showing 10, a marvellous vision of Jesus' heart, wounded and emptied out as a place where all of humanity can find solace and joy:

> Then with a glad expression our Lord looked into his side and gazed, rejoicing; and with his dear gaze he led his creature's understanding through the same wound into his side within. And then he revealed a beautiful and delightful place, large enough for all mankind that shall be saved to rest there in peace and in love. (BW, LT 24)

In the account of Jesus' death in John's Gospel a soldier is said to have pierced Jesus' side with a spear to ensure his death, and blood and water flowed out from this wound. This small detail at the end of the Passion story in one of the Gospels became a focus for Christian devotion. Julian taps into this devotional tradition as she continues reflecting on the heart 'riven in two'.

> [W]ith that [God] brought to mind his beloved blood and precious water which he let pour all out for love. And with the precious vision he showed his blessed heart quite riven in

two. And with this sweet rejoicing he revealed in part to my understanding the blessed Godhead ... strengthening then the poor soul to understand, as far as it may be expressed ... the meaning of the endless love which was without beginning, and is, and always shall be. And with this our good Lord said most blessedly, 'Look how I loved you' ... (BW, LT 24)

A devotional reading of Julian might adopt this image of Jesus' open heart as an image to be contemplated and in which we can find peace. The heart cut open is itself a vivid expression of God's vulnerability to us, and the emptiness of Jesus' heart is an expression of God having poured out Godself to make room for us within God's own life. There is a record of human violence here, but also of divine love using our violence to make a home for all of us in God. We can also easily apply the image back to ourselves: the piercing wounds we have endured in life, and the self-emptying loss and grief that we have endured, can serve to make us more open to others, more sensitive and more empathic. But for this to happen we need the courage to accept our wounds and then the faith to offer them to God, and the patience to wait for transformation. Gazing on Jesus dying from his wounds, and gazing on the risen Jesus with his unbroken love for us in spite of his suffering, gives us this kind of spiritual courage and steadfastness. Faith works in these simple ways, with the material of our lives already at hand, and learning to be faithful means learning these simple, humble ways of bringing our self-awareness together with our awareness of God.

Showing 11: Discovering Community

In the next chapter, the Showings continue with Julian having a vision of the Blessed Virgin Mary in heaven.

And with this same expression of gladness and joy our good Lord looked down on his right side and brought to my mind where our Lady stood during his Passion, and he said, 'Would you like to see her?' ... as if he had said, 'Would you like to see how I love her, so that you can rejoice with me in the love that I have for her and she for me?' (BW, LT 25)

Part of heaven, for Julian, is our enjoyment of how much *others* are loved, and how much *others* are blessed, and even how God created some to be more blessed to look at than we are ourselves! Jesus thus asks Julian:

'Would you like to see in her *how you are loved*? For love *of you* I made her so exalted, so noble, and of such worth; and this delights me, and I want it to delight you.' For after himself [Julian continues] *she is the most blessed sight.* (BW, LT 25, emphasis mine)

For Julian, being in God was inherently communal, and part of our delight in this heavenly family is delighting in how *others* are loved, and delighting too at our inclusion in a communion in which others are created to be even more delightful than we are. This is the opposite of envy: the celebration of each other, in which we can rest assured in others' delight in us. It's like discovering ourselves in a great cascading chain of delight and blessedness, overflowing with others' delight in us and passing it on to others.

Our faith in this communion of joy in God, in which we are completely welcome, can loosen the resentment we have around our own shortcomings and failures, or the shortcomings of life as a whole. On the one hand, we can be honest about our feelings of failure and loss, but, on the other, we can savour the blessedness of others who include us in their joy, just as we are.

Showing 12: Passing Beyond Words

Showing 12 is a fitting end to these heavenly Showings, and our journey through the first twelve Showings as a whole. In this Showing, Julian experiences God's glory in a litany of divine joy and self-offering that spills over into exalted silence.

And after this our Lord showed himself yet more glorified, as it seemed to me, than I had seen him before ... Our Lord Jesus often said, 'It is I. It is I. It is I who am highest. It is I you love. It is I you delight in. It is I you serve. It is I you long for. It is I you desire. It is I who am your purpose. It is I who am all ... It is I who showed myself to you here.' The number of words transcended my wits and all my understanding, and all my powers, for they are most exalted, as it seems to me, for I cannot tell what they comprehend; but the joy that I saw when they were revealed surpasses all that heart may wish and soul may desire. (BW, LT 26)

Julian is taken up and lost in the delight that God is. 'It is I ... It is I ... !' She ends the chapter simply with a prayer that we might be able to receive and experience what she cannot express:

And therefore the words [given inwardly to her in this Showing] are not explained here; but may everyone, according to the grace that God gives him in understanding and loving, receive them as our Lord intended. (BW, LT 26)

Considering the Journey thus Far

From this high and exalted point, as we conclude the first part of this book and before we begin a more reflective and questioning second stage in our journey through the *Revelations*, it might help to look back, as from a mountain top, to see the journey we have already travelled.

We started with Julian's desire to live closer to God, more faithful to Jesus, and to be wounded with compassion, contrition and longing.

We then read Julian's description of her near-death illness, in which she oscillates between life and death, and which ends with the stunning realization *that just by living ordinary human life* she can experience compassion with Jesus, and thus be intimately in touch with God. Being surrendered and open in ordinary life is Julian's way of being surrendered and open to God.

The Showings proper then began with a double showing of Jesus in his Passion and the Trinity in joy, thus putting Julian in touch with suffering humanity – her humanity, Jesus' humanity, all of humanity – and in touch with an eternal happiness, an internal affirmation of all in joy.

Showings 2 and 3 explored this experience in strikingly different ways, Showing 2 asking us to believe we are continually experiencing God, even in suffering, and Showing 3 challenging our ordinary human judgement with a vision of God rejoicing unconditionally in everything.

Showings 4, 5 and 6 elaborated aspects of Julian's faith in Jesus and his Passion, and in Showing 7 Julian shares the volatility of her spiritual experience.

In Showing 8, the crisis and pivot on which the first part of Julian's story turns, we journeyed with Julian into the suffering humanity of Jesus, and witnessed as Julian's faith, grounded in compassionate openness to Jesus, self and others, was both tested and unconditionally confirmed.

This led into a series of joyous Showings, 9 to 12, which we have just reviewed.

In terms of our journey into faith, all the major pieces of what this faith is are now in front of us. It is a faith that, in its disciplined openness to everyday human experience *and* to a revelation of God's love in Jesus, allows ourselves, our world and the word of God's love to come into contact within us. Faith is not just a set of beliefs or a feeling of trust, but a courageous welcoming and surrender of self that allows our lives and our world to come into contact with God's love and to be changed by this.

We have seen already indications of what blocks this process: our wrathfulness at how life is, a wrath that rejects ourselves, our world, and God's word of love. Spiritual maturation comes in the slaking and satisfying of such wrath by prayer, meditation and increasing knowledge of self and God.

There are of course questions remaining. How could a loving God have allowed our suffering and sin in the first place? How could a loving God rejoice in a world where there is such suffering and sin? And how is our wrath calmed? How is our resentment eased, such that the hurt in our lives can come into contact with God's hurt for us, and thus move towards healing?

These are exactly the questions that Julian explores in the next stage of our journey, Part Two of this book, and Chapters 27–51 of the *Revelations*.

Questions for Reflection and Discussion

1 What old wounds do you have from past life experiences, old grief, old pain, old loss? What new wounds have you experienced today: fresh anger, fresh frustration, fresh betrayal? What is the feeling of these wounds? Can you hold them in your mind and *at the same time* hold a mental image of Jesus with his wounds – welcoming and delighting in all of us?

2 We all have people in life who have shown us love, or courage, or admiration, or respect. Who have these people been for you? When you think back to those experiences of being loved and admired, what do you feel was given to you?

3 Slowly recite the litany of divine affirmation from Julian's twelfth Showing. Pause and recite it again. Recite it for as long as it seems soothing or beneficial. Ask God to open your heart and mind to its meaning.

> It is I.
> It is I.
> It is I who am highest.
> It is I you love.
> It is I you delight in.
> It is I you serve.
> It is I you long for.
> It is I you desire.
> It is I who am your purpose.
> It is I who am all.
> It is I that Holy Church preaches and teaches you.
> It is I who showed myself to you here.

What phrase stands out, rings with the most meaning? If you repeat this one phrase quietly to yourself, listening to it speak and resound within yourself, what emerges?

PART TWO

Julian's Questioning: The Critical Testing and Deepening of Faith

All Shall Be Well. Really?

If the last three-quarters of Julian's *Revelations of Divine Love* had been lost, the first part, containing the first 12 Showings, would have seemed like a complete story that begins with Julian's illness, continues through a middle section building to crisis at Showing 8, and ends with a satisfying conclusion in Showing 12, with Julian lapsing into mystical awe and peace.

Yet the *Revelations* do in fact go on, for 60 more chapters – chapters 27 to 86! In these chapters, Julian reports less on direct mystical experience and engages more in critical questioning and reflection about what she has already experienced.

Why Did God Allow Sin and Suffering?

As Julian describes it, what draws her out of the mystical reverie she enjoyed at the end of Showing 12 was an awareness of how much she had previously suffered from frustrated longing for God.

> After this, the Lord brought to mind the longing that I had for him before; and I saw that nothing held me back except sin, and I saw that this is so with all of us in general. And it seemed to me that if there had been no sin, we should all have been pure and like our Lord, as he made us; and so, in my folly, I had often wondered before this time why, through the great foreseeing wisdom of God, the beginning of sin was not pre-vented ... I should have given up such thoughts, yet I grieved and sorrowed over this, unreasonably and without discretion. (BW, LT 27)

In Showing 3, Julian had wondered briefly about the reality of sin and set it aside in order to surrender herself to God's joy; but now, in a slightly different form, Julian's perplexity about sin and suffering returns with a vengeance. How can she square her experience of a God of unconstrained love and intimate friendship with her experience of so much sin and suffering in human life? Julian has already found solace and security in the God of compassion who shares all her experience with her, but why had God not prevented suffering in the first place?

It is important to clarify that when Julian talks about 'sin', she is not speaking merely of moral failure. 'Sin' for Julian indicates such failures, but also includes all the physical, psychological and social pains that we experience, and which she saw most vividly portrayed in Jesus' death:

[Sin is] everything in general which is not good, and the shameful scorn and the uttermost abnegation that he bore for us in this life, and his dying, and all the pains and sufferings in body and spirit of all his creations – for we are all in part set at nought ... (BW, LT 27)

Thus 'grieving and sorrowing without discretion', about the wrongness and suffering in creation on every possible level, Julian is now far from the mystical satisfaction that she enjoyed at the end of Showing 12. She is anxious, she is pained, and we could say that in this passage she is voicing resentment against God for allowing so much suffering.

All Shall Be Well

What follows from Julian's pained questioning is the most famous passage in the entire *Revelations of Divine Love* and perhaps the most famous saying in English spirituality as a whole. Jesus answers Julian:

'Sin is befitting, but all shall be well, and all shall be well, and all manner of things shall be well.' (BW, LT 27)

Later, God reiterates the divine promise of a universal making well of all things:

> It's true [God says to Julian] that sin is the cause of all this suffering, but all shall be well and all shall be well, and all manner of things shall be well. (BW, LT 27)

Words that Effect what They Say

Having worked alongside the Julian Shrine in Norwich, and having lived for many years in a monastery that celebrated Julian as its patron, I cannot deny how these four simple words, 'all shall be well', have had a profound effect on countless people. As mentioned in the introduction to this book, I have met any number of people who, knowing nothing about Julian, were introduced to 'all shall be well' in moments of crisis and for whom the phrase proved profoundly healing. For some the words are sacramental, catalysing the spiritual wellness of which they speak.

And yet for Julian herself, as for many of us, the words do not provide immediate consolation, but confusion. How could God ever make all things well, really? Isn't the suffering of the world, isn't the suffering of my own life, too vast and horrible for that? Thus, after God says 'All shall be well' to Julian, she then proceeds to argue with God for many chapters about how this could not possibly be the case!

Showing 13, spanning 13 chapters, is largely a conversation between Julian and God about the possibility of all being made well. Thus, even as God invites Julian to trust in God's promise to make all things well, Julian counters God by bringing up further reasons why all things could not possibly be made well. She holds up, for instance, the great harm done to creation by sin (LT 29), and, a few chapters later, she presents the Church's teaching regarding eternal damnation. How could the eternal suffering of some creatures be part of a universe where all manner of things is made well?

And considering all this [how the Church teaches about the eternal condemnation of some to hell], it seemed impossible to me that all manner of things should be well, as our Lord revealed at this time. (BW, LT 32)

The fact that Julian does argue with God, and does struggle with *all shall be well*, gives us permission to struggle seriously with whether we ourselves can authentically believe this and inhabit it, and what such believing might mean. Can we look at our lives, and the lives of those around us, and the history of the world, and really affirm *everything* as involved in a process of well-making? Can we really be that universally open and acceptant to what is? Is this a responsible way to live? Is it helpful?

All Shall Be Well Present Throughout the Showings

For Julian, she has to come to terms with *all shall be well* because it articulates the heart of what she has experienced of God all through the *Revelations*.

In Showing 1, Julian shared with us her vision of a homely God who in love is the ground of all being, who encloses all and cherishes all. This God is present in all things, and loves all things, and is present even in drastic creaturely suffering and human tragedy.

In Showing 2, Julian shares with us God's desire for us to believe that we are experiencing God continually, even if this is completely obscured by suffering. All experience is open to God and is included in Jesus' redemptive love.

In Showing 3, God invites Julian to share in God's unconditional affirmation and joy in all things, with God being in all things and doing all that is done. This is very, very close to the kind of state that Julian is challenged to live into in 'all shall be well'.

In Showing 8, Julian's fidelity to God, as present in Jesus, is tested in terms of her willingness to stay with Jesus as her heaven in suffering and joy. Julian accepts without conditions her human, earthly experience as the medium through which her relationship with God is deepened and God's work is being done. All things are included in this.

Finally, in Showing 9, Julian and we her readers are faced with the searching question, whether we can be satisfied with God's way of loving us in the person of Jesus, redeeming our lives not by re-creating heaven and earth more to our liking, but making our actual experience the means for a relationship of compassionate intimacy and companionship.

All through the Showings Julian has thus been invited to widen her love, to deepen her acceptance and, increasingly, to accept absolutely all things as the place of God's presence, God's redemptive work and God's rejoicing. At the very end of the *Revelations*, Julian even returns to 'all shall be well' to make it key to her sense of heaven:

> When the judgement is given and we are all brought up above [to heaven], then shall we clearly see in God the secrets which are now hidden from us. Then shall none of us be moved to say in any way: 'Lord, if it had been thus-and-so, then it would have been all well'; but we shall say all in one voice: 'Lord, blessed mayest Thou be! Because it is as it is; it is well. And now we see truly that everything is done as was Thine ordinance before anything was made.' (JJS, LT 85)

The journey of Julian's faith is thus a journey towards this unqualified affirmation: 'Because it is as it is, it is well.'

What is at stake then in our questioning of 'all shall be well' is in fact an elementary spiritual and religious choice, itself at the heart of Julian's spirituality. Do we live in a world where some things must be rejected as outside God's power to redeem, where religion must cast some things out, or do we live in a world where God is present and at work, without constraints, in all things, to make all well? If we choose the former, then faith and spirituality tilts towards maintaining a purity of self, or a purity of community, over against an excluded 'darkness'. If we choose the latter, then spirituality and Christian faith becomes a process in which God works with us to gradually widen our acceptance of all things as being the place where God is active, and God's redeeming presence can be known. Moreover, we become places where God's love touches the world with compassion and cherishing. The Kingdom of God is within and between us, and nothing is, from the start, excluded. This, we might say, is a truly universal or catholic faith.

The Secrets of God and a Life of Unknowing

In response to her sharp questioning, God extends to Julian many assurances over several chapters of Showing 13, that all, really *all* things, are going to be made well. God also provides Julian with examples that seem to show this well-making at work, if in a partial way. God reminds Julian, for instance, how the sins of the saints are recognized now as part of their glory, because these sins are looked on as wounds the saints suffered in spiritual battle and reveal, furthermore, the healing mercy and transformative goodness of God (see LT 38). In a similar way we can be aware, years after an apparently unredeemable tragedy or moral failing, that profound goodness eventually came from it.

In the end, however, God does not *explain* to Julian, literally, how the suffering and tragedy of creation is going to be made well. What God does, over and over again, is to invite Julian to trust in this, to be increasingly open to life in this truth, *even though she can't understand or perceive how it could ever be so.*

Julian says in fact that God showed her that there are two parts to God's saving work. One is open and knowable, and in it we can grow through the faith of the Church and inner experience. But there is another aspect to God's working that is hidden from us, not because we are slow to understand, but because God wants to keep it hidden!

One [part] is our Saviour and our salvation. This blessed part is open and clear, and fair and light and abundant ... We are bound to this by God, and drawn and counselled and taught, inwardly by the Holy Spirit, and outwardly by Holy Church, through the same grace. Our Lord wants us to be occupied with this, rejoicing in him for he rejoices in us. (BW, LT 30)

The other part is hidden and barred to us ... for this is our Lord's private counsels, and it is fitting for the royal lordship of God to keep his private counsels undisturbed ... (BW, LT 30)

Julian conceives that our appropriate response to these divine secrets is *not* to try to work them out.

[I]t is fitting for the royal lordship of God to keep his private counsels undisturbed, and it is fitting for his servant, out of obedience and respect, not to wish to know his counsels.

This may sound harsh, too much like a peasant cringing before a king. Why can't God tell us what God is about? But Julian suggests that we damage ourselves spiritually when we try to work this out and that it is *out of love* that God has not shown this secret to us.

Our Lord has pity and compassion on us, because some people busy themselves so anxiously about this; and I am sure that if we knew how much we should please [God] and set our minds at rest by leaving it alone, we would do so. (BW, LT 30)

Living All Shall Be Well, this Side of Heaven

Where this leaves us is in a very delicate spiritual position, but one that is full of promise, one that describes a new way of life.

On the one hand, we are invited to live into an assurance of all things being made well. Nothing is out of the reach of God's working. This means living with a radical openness to all things as having God at work in them to make them well.

But on the other hand, in many cases, big and small, personal and historical, we can't possibly see how this could be the case; it is even an affront to our suffering to pretend that we can. And as Julian has made clear, this is not because we aren't perceptive or clever or spiritual enough, it is because God has freely chosen *not* to make known the 'Great Deed' by which all will be made well. Furthermore, we damage ourselves if we attempt to spin theories that can explain this universal well-making.

We are left then in a interesting state: increasingly open to all things in the *assumption* that God is at work within them, but also feeling keenly at times that we can't understand how this could be so.

On reflection, this seems like an honest and courageous way to live, in touch with reality because open in trust to its essential goodness – not having to cut it down to fit into a pre-planned theological understanding. We can be present to the suffering and even the wrongness in our lives with greater curiosity and tenderness. We can trust that all is already included in God's universal well-making, and thus we can increasingly accept it, but we don't have to work out how it might be redeemed. This might be described as a state of openness, sensitivity and assurance, which proceeds in trust and, at times, touches mysteriously on something of God's joy.

Questions for Reflection and Discussion

1   Have you come across 'all shall be well' already in your life? What has it meant to you?
2   Reflecting over your personal life (not the tragic events of world history!), make a list of a few things that you can't see ever being made well. There are tragedies in each of our lives that don't seem open to redemption. Invite one of these into your awareness, and invite in God's promise that this too will be made well. You are placing these experiences before God, and God is saying that they will be made well. What is it like to do this? What feelings arise? What in you resists this? What in you finds joy in this?
3   What is it like for you to be told that God is explicitly keeping 'a secret' from you and, for your benefit, is suggesting

that you should not try to work this out – suggesting in fact that the more you try to figure it out, the further you will be from living with it? Can you believe that trying to work this out would be harmful to you? Why or why not? Are you comfortable living with this unknowing, a kind of incomprehension in which all the truths of life cannot finally be integrated?

12

The Slaking of our Wrath

Not Desiring All Things to Be Well

In the last chapter we saw that Julian accepts that we can't understand how all things could ever be made well; God has chosen not to reveal this to us. Julian invites us nonetheless to trust 'all shall be well' as a basic truth that encourages a great openness and sensitivity to self and world.

Beyond not being able to *understand* how all things could be made well, there is, however, another, more serious obstacle to making 'all shall be well' our own. This is the fact that we don't *want* some things to be made well. We don't want some parts of ourselves, or events in our lives, or world history, ever to be included in God's universal well-making. We want some things in our lives, or in the world's life, to be permanently damned – which is to say excluded and punished or simply destroyed in God's proverbial 'lake of fire'. The only way there can be heaven, or unqualified wellness, for us is, it seems, for other things to be eternally condemned, excluded from our reality, perhaps destroyed.

This resistance to God's universal well-making is what Julian calls our *wrath*, and it's this wrath that needs to be healed if we are to be fully reconciled to ourselves and our world, and transformed in God. In Chapters 46–49, perhaps the most theologically and therapeutically significant of the *Revelations*, Julian explores God's saving work in healing our wrath, and what happens with us as we are healed.

There Is No Wrath in God

To begin, there is for many nothing more shocking in the *Revelations* than Julian's pronouncement in Chapter 46 that there is no wrath in God, a viewpoint that she unfolds systematically. She starts by sharing her earlier agreement with the standard religious perspective of her time, that God responds to our sin with both anger and blame:

> [I]t seemed necessary to me to see and to recognize that we are sinners and do many evil things that we ought to avoid, and leave many good deeds undone that we ought to do, and for this we deserve pain, blame, and anger. (BW, LT 46)

Julian, however, renounces all of this, because she saw no anger in God, and what she did see in God seemed directly opposite to anger or blame:

> And in spite of all this [the Church's teaching of her time], I saw truly that our Lord was never angry, nor ever shall be, for he is God: he is good, he is truth, he is love, he is peace; and his power, his wisdom, his charity, and his unity do not permit him to be angry ... God is the goodness that cannot be angry, for he is nothing but goodness. (BW, LT 46)

> [T]o the soul which through his special grace sees so much of the great and wonderful goodness of God – and that we are endlessly united to him in love – it is the greatest impossibility there could be that God should be angry, for anger and friendship are two opposites. (BW, LT 49)

Because Julian experienced God as one who in loving, intimate friendship suffers with us, she can't imagine a God reared up against us in flaring anger. She goes on:

> It must necessarily be so that he who dispels and destroys our anger and makes us meek and mild is himself always constant

in love, meek and mild, which is the opposite of anger. For I saw very clearly that where our Lord appears, peace reigns, and anger has no place. (BW, LT 49)

To imagine God as angry with us for what we do is to imagine a God who is *in competition with us* for how history will turn out, and whose plans are in danger of being permanently ruined by us. Such an image of God is completely incompatible with Julian's vision of God's unconditional and joyous assurance of all being made well. Julian's God certainly suffers hurt with us when we hurt ourselves and others by sin, and it is perhaps tempting to speak of a God who is angry with us for hurting ourselves. But even this is not admissible for Julian, since for her God is already experiencing the joy and goodness that God shall make out of all things, even our sin.

In one last step, Julian even argues metaphysically, going back to the great hazelnut vision in Showing 1. Since God's loving of us is the ground of our being, if God ever were really angry with us, we would simply cease to exist:

... for truly, as it seems to me, if God could be angry even for an instant we should never have life, nor place, *nor being*; for as truly as we have our being from the endless power of God, and from the endless wisdom, and from the endless goodness, so truly we have our safekeeping in the endless power of God, in the endless wisdom, and in the endless goodness. (BW, LT 49, emphasis mine)

Julian's sense that there is no anger or blame in God is not a passing phenomenon but is something, she says, to which her 'soul was led by love and powerfully drawn in every revelation' (BW, LT 46).

The Wrath that Is in Us

Asserting that there is no wrath in God created, however, another problem for Julian: if there is no divine wrath, what then is the role of divine mercy and forgiveness? If we take away God's wrath, our entire theology must be transformed.

> I contemplated and wondered very much what the mercy and forgiveness of God is; for according to the teaching that I received earlier, I understood that the mercy of God would be the remission of his anger after occasions when we have sinned. For it seemed to me that to a soul whose intention and desire is to love, the anger of God would be harder than any other pain, and therefore I took it that the remission of his anger would be one of the principal features of his mercy. But however much I might look and long I could not see this anywhere in the entire revelation. (BW, LT 47)

Julian's solution, so radical for her day, so apt for our own, is that while there is no wrath in God, there is in fact a great deal of wrath in us:

> I saw no anger except on man's part, and [God] forgives that in us; for anger is nothing else but a resistance and contrariness to peace and to love, and it comes either from lack of strength, or from lack of wisdom, or from lack of goodness – and this lack is not in God, but it is on our part; for through sin and wretchedness we have in us a wretched and continual resistance to peace and to love, and [God] revealed this very often in his loving expression of pity and compassion. (BW, LT 48)

The problem is not merely that we from time to time get angry, or have a bad temper, or can't be as loving as God wants us to be. Rather, we have in us a 'wretched and continual resistance to peace and to love'. We have in us a warring against God, expressed at times in our desire that God would not make some things well, our desire that God would in fact be angry and condemning.

God Slaking Our Wrath

The drama of Christian salvation, in these brief chapters, is thus turned on its head. No longer is it about us behaving well to stay in God's good graces, or God, because of Jesus' Passion, allowing us into heaven. The wrath that blocks us from heaven is in us, not God; and divine mercy, and Jesus' Passion, works to slake our wrath and our sense of justice, not God's.

About our human condition, Julian writes:

[M]an is changeable in this life, and falls into sin through frailty and being overcome; in himself he is weak and foolish, and also his will is overwhelmed, and during this time he is in turmoil, and in sorrow and misery. (BW, LT 47)

Yet in our blindness and foolishness, we are still protected by God:

And though we, through the anger and contrary spirit that is within us, are now in tribulation, distress, and misery, as befits our blindness and weakness, yet we are certainly safe through the merciful protection of God, so that we do not perish. (BW, LT 49)

... [and] the same endless goodness that protects us when we sin so that we do not perish, that same endless goodness continually effects a peace in us to set against our anger and our perverse falling ... for we cannot be blessedly saved until we are truly in a state of peace and love; for that is our salvation. (BW, LT 49)

Our salvation, to which all of God's working is bent, is in being brought to a state beyond wrath, a state of peace and love. Julian goes on to spell out just how unconditional our acceptance and contentment, our wrathless-ness, must be:

[W]e are not blessedly safe in the possession of our endless joy until we are all in peace and in love: that is to say, in full contentment with God, and with all his works, and with all his judgements, and loving and at peace with ourselves and with our fellow Christians and with all that God loves, as is pleasing to love. (BW, LT 49)

This is describing a state of complete surrender and complete acceptance. Once our wrath is slaked in this way, even temporarily, we suddenly find ourselves, Julian says, already one with God:

I saw that God is our true peace, and our sure protector when we are not at peace in ourselves, and he works continually to bring us into endless peace. And so when we, through the working of mercy and grace, are made humble and gentle, we are completely safe. Suddenly the soul is united to God when it is truly at peace in itself, for no anger is to be found in God. (BW, LT 49)

How God Works: In Jesus and the Holy Spirit

Theologically, Julian is in agreement with traditional Christian theology in believing that there are two basic ways in which God works with us to slake our wrath.

First, God works to slake our wrath in the person of Jesus of Nazareth, who is a revelation, the incarnate Word, of God's love and compassion in a human being, as something objective that we encounter in the history of the world. As we gaze on this Jesus, we are in the presence of a God who loves us unconditionally and who, open to our suffering, chooses always to remain open to us and all our experience. There is this infinite tenderness at the heart of the cosmos, tenderness and desire for us and our joy, and for Julian this is expressed in the person, life and death of Jesus.

The essential religious and spiritual moment is when this incarnate love eases the wrath we have in us towards part of ourselves, or towards life, or towards God in Godself. We are able to accept more of ourselves, one another and God because we have a sense of being accompanied by this divine tenderness and care and compassion. Julian is well aware of how fallen the Church is, but she still sees its role as continuing through the centuries to reveal the love that Jesus is, ideally in the kind and compassionate nature of the Christian community itself.

> [T]hen I saw that each instance of kind compassion that a man feels for his fellow Christians out of love – it is Christ in him ... [Christ] wants us to know that [all suffering] will all be turned to glory and advantage by virtue of his Passion, and to know that we do not suffer alone but with him, and to see in him our foundation, and to see that his pains and his self-abnegation so far surpass all that we may suffer that it cannot be fully comprehended. (BW, LT 28)

The second manner of God's working with us in our wrath is in the Holy Spirit, who Julian understands as always at work in us, not as something we encounter 'out there' in history like the teaching, actions and crucifixion of Jesus, but love present mysteriously within us, working on our subjective state from within. The Holy Spirit, for Julian, is God secretly present to us, sometimes without our awareness, soothing our anger, our terror, our pain and grief, so that we can open again to peace and love:

> [O]ur good Lord, the Holy Spirit, who is endless life dwelling in our soul, protects us most securely, and effects a peace in the soul, and gives it comfort by grace, and accords it to God, and makes it compliant. And this is his mercy and the path on which our Lord continually leads us, as long as we are in this changeable life. (BW, LT 48)

Conclusion: Our Salvation Worked Out in Daily Life

Julian's theological vision of how God saves us is simple, profound and coherent as it radiates through all the fields of Christian understanding. It is as if Julian has 'demythologized' the process of our healing and salvation, revealing the problem (our wrath) and the processes by which God is directly at work in our lives to heal this.

Our Christian faith, which we have previously described as a sustained openness to ourselves, the world and God's word of love, revealed in Jesus, so that all these touch within us, is the *facilitative condition* of God's being able to work with us in love for our healing, transformation and increasing resonance with God's light and love and life.

The place where such a faith-journey is engaged is none other than daily life. Daily life, with its sheer unpredictability, its stresses and pains, its raptures and delights, is the place where God works with us. It's here that our proverbial 'buttons' are pushed, where we feel the hurt of the wrath that is still in us. We remain out of control of our daily lives, and it's this lack of control that allows God to stir up, through trivial and traumatic events alike, everything in us that needs, not just God's loving attention, but our loving attention and our loving care. When we allow our awareness to rest on our hurt, our anger, our grief, we are co-workers with God, allowing God more extensive presence in our lives.

Questions for Reflection and Discussion

1 Can you imagine living with a God in whom there is no wrath? Do you want God to be angry because this seems more just, less ethereal and more real? Or might you want God's wrath to support condemnation of parts of yourself, your life or the world? Can you give voice to what you feel when you imagine God not being wrathful and condemning?

2 Julian describes God slaking our wrath through the offer of love and compassion in Jesus of Nazareth, and secretly, inwardly, in the work of the Holy Spirit.

(1) How important is Jesus in your life of faith? Can you imagine a deeper devotion to him, a deeper listening to him? What would this look like in practice? Might it be in a Bible study group, a personal reading of Scripture, a daily journal conversation with Jesus in your imagination, or daily prayer or attendance at church? How can you more generously welcome Jesus, as the image and word and revelation of God's love, into your inner life?

(2) The Holy Spirit is always, already, at work in you, attempting to ease your wrath and pain. Are there any spiritual practices that help you to release yourself to this divine presence, this flow of God's Spirit? Have you experienced this in meditation or contemplative prayer, formally or informally? Have you experienced something like this in nature, or with friends, or interacting with art?

3 Think back to an experience in daily life when suddenly you were overwhelmed with anger or frustration or despair. These happen to many of us daily! Go back to the difficult experience and, in faith, invite it into your awareness. Can you show the experience not scorn, not condemnation, not embarrassment, but loving attention and accepting care? What was happening for you and others in that moment? Can you let the anger or despair or frustration speak more? What would it say?

13

Prayer Unites the Soul to God

Introduction: A Showing on Prayer

Julian's most sustained reflection on prayer happens in Showing 14, Chapters 41–43 of the *Revelations*. Beginning with God's response to her insecurity about prayer, Julian reflects theoretically on what prayer is and how it comes about, and she shares with us something of her personal experience of prayer. While not providing a systematic treatise on prayer, let alone a particular method of praying, these chapters give us the chance to encounter Julian most personally, and to deepen our understanding of prayer as the heart of the life of faith.

'I Am the Foundation of Your Prayers'

Julian begins the Showing with a confession of difficulties in prayer:

> [O]ur trust [in our praying] is often not complete, for it seems to us that, because of our unworthiness and because we feel nothing at all, we are not sure that God hears us. For often we are as barren and dry after our prayers as we were before, and when we feel like this our folly is the cause of our weakness. For I have felt this way myself. (BW, LT 41)

We, like Julian, can be insecure in our praying. We are not sure anyone is there to hear us. Nothing seems to happen as a result of our prayers; sometimes we don't even feel better.

And our Lord brought all this suddenly to mind and revealed these words and said, 'I am the foundation of your prayers: first, it is my will that you should have something, and then I make you desire it, and then I make you pray for it ... how then could it be that you should not have what you pray for?' (BW, LT 41)

As the foundation of our prayer, the desires that God stirs up in us are not desires for just anything, as Julian says later, but are very specifically desires for 'mercy and grace' (LT 41). The desire that God creates in us is for God's life to flow into us for our healing and protection (mercy) and for our growth and transformation (grace).

Mercy works – protecting, tolerating, reviving, and healing, and all through the tenderness of love; and grace works: raising, rewarding, and endlessly exceeding what our love and our efforts deserve ... grace transforms our shameful falling into a high and honourable rising ... our sorrowful dying into holy, blessed life. (BW, LT 48)

Prayer is thus our cooperation with God's desire to heal us and make us new. It begins with God, and involves us as active partners in receiving and cooperating with God, and spills over from us into the world. God wishes to heal us; in our praying, we are making that wish our own and giving God deeper access to our lives. We pray so that God can change us, not the other way round.

For when the soul is in turmoil, troubled, and alone in its distress, then it is time to pray, to make itself compliant and submissive to God. But no kind of prayer makes God compliant to the soul, because God's love is always the same. (BW, LT 43)

Prayer in Dryness

The fact that in prayer we are not trying to change God or make God compliant with us, but are rather yielding ourselves and our world to God, is why it's not primarily significant how we feel in our prayers, or after them. It might be that all that we have to yield to God's mercy and grace is our suffering, our emptiness, or the world's pain, even our feeling of divine absence.

The success of such prayer, if such a thing can be said, is only that we have intended to yield ourselves and our world to God, intended to be responsive and cooperative with God's desire, which is, after all, already a sign of God's working in us. This is why Julian perceives God as saying:

> Pray with all your heart, even though you may feel nothing, though you may see nothing – yes, even though you may think you cannot. For in dryness and in barrenness, in sickness and in weakness, then your prayers are most pleasing to me, even though it seems to you that they give you almost no pleasure. And so it is in my sight with all your faithful prayers. (BW, LT 41)

Prayer in these conditions is most pleasing to God as the naked intention to remain tender and compassionate to what is most difficult in ourselves and our world, and also to be compassionate and responsive to God's desire – we might say even God's painful yearning – to bring healing. This is the bare essence and realization of the life of faith.

> And sometimes when the heart is dry and feels nothing, or else through temptation by our enemy, then it is driven by reason and by grace to cry out to our Lord aloud, recounting his blessed Passion and his great goodness. And the power of our Lord's word enters the soul and gives life to the heart, and through his grace causes it to work truly, making it pray very blessedly and truly to rejoice in our Lord. (BW, LT 41)

Prayer Unites the Soul to God

Because Julian conceives of prayer not as a desperate striving to change or get to God, but as a yielding of ourselves to what God desires, it is easy to understand why she sees prayer as what reconciles us to God and allows us to share in God's own life. Julian says:

> Prayer is a true, gracious, lasting will of the soul united and joined to the will of our Lord by the precious and mysterious working of the Holy Spirit. (BW, LT 41)

As we open ourselves and our world to God's mercy, our wrathful contrariness to God is eased and as a result we find ourselves falling naturally into resonance with God. This is the mysterious work of God's Spirit. And as we open ourselves to Grace, we find a new life bubbling up through what had seemed like death.

> [T]hrough his grace [God] makes us like himself in condition as we are in nature, and this is his blessed will. (BW, LT 41)

> Prayer unites the soul to God; for though the soul is always like God in nature and substance, restored by grace, it is often unlike him in condition, through sin on man's part. Then prayer is a witness that the soul wills as God wills, and eases the conscience and fits man to receive grace. (BW, LT 43)

There are, furthermore, moments when, for Julian, God shows Godself to us more openly, and in this prayer it seems we almost forget ourselves and find our joy in moving just as God moves, surrendered to him:

> But when our courteous Lord shows himself to our soul through his grace, we have what we desire, and for a while we do not see what we should pray for, but our whole aim and all our strength is set entirely on the contemplation of him. And this is an exalted, imperceptible prayer, as it seems to me; for

the whole reason why we pray is to be at one with the sight and contemplation of him to whom we pray, experiencing a marvellous rejoicing, with reverent fear and such great sweetness and delight in him that we can only pray as [God] moves us at the time. (BW, LT 43)

Such prayer is a foretaste of heaven, which Julian describes with remarkable sensuality:

[W]e shall, by his precious grace, in our own humble and continued prayers, come into [God] now in this life through many mysterious touches of precious spiritual revelations and feelings ... until we shall die in longing for love. And then we shall all enter into our Lord, knowing ourselves clearly and possessing God in full; and we will be unendingly and wholly possessed in God, seeing him truly and feeling him fully, hearing him spiritually, and smelling him delectably, and swallowing him sweetly. And then we shall see God face to face, intimately and fully. (BW, LT 43)

Conclusion: Living in Tenderness and Compassion

Julian's vision of the spiritual life is a vision of human beings living increasingly surrendered and moved by the love that God is. Faith means engaging in the process directly, because faith, as we have seen, is that primordial openness to self, the world and God, and it is precisely this openness that gives God further ability to heal us, uniting how we are in daily life with how God is. Prayer, understood as a discrete activity done at particular times, is our conscious choice to enter into our faith, practising tenderness and compassion to ourselves, to others and to God in God's own desiring love. In prayer, we choose to be tender and compassionate, and thus responsive, not only to ourselves and the world, but to God and God's desire to heal and transform our world. It's as if our desire, and the world's need, and God's desire meet and dovetail within us. The more our lives are thus drawn into harmony with God's life, the more our living itself becomes prayer, and we approach the state of 'unceasing prayer' that St Paul spoke of and which has been the focus of great swathes of Christian spiritual writing for centuries.

Questions for Reflection and Discussion

1 Describe your life of prayer as it is now. How do you attempt to remain open to yourself, your world and God so that these can meet within you and touch on one another?

2 Does your prayer life tend more towards knowing yourself, for example in introspection, therapy and journal writing, or more towards knowing God, for example in Scripture study, theology and meditation, or more towards knowing the world, for instance in the arts or politics or news? Or do you tend more towards letting go of self and world in quiet resting in God; that is, towards a more contemplative spirituality? Does there need to be a rebalancing of these different aspects of prayer for you? How might that be addressed practically?

3 Does your prayer life lead to action in the world? Does it lead to a more concrete and specific sense of your way of following Jesus' tenderness and truthfulness and justice in your life and community?

4 Julian writes honestly about a sense of barrenness and futility in prayer as well as exuberantly about being touched by God and feelings and inspirations of the divine. Would you want to be this open to God, this vulnerable to feelings of divine presence and absence? Might it seem like a more passionate life, or just a less stable one? Where does Julian find her stability amid her changing feelings?

14

There is a Lord with a Mysterious Servant

Throughout the *Revelations*, we have seen that Julian experiences God as having no wrath at our sins and, what is more, not even *blaming* us for them. For instance, at the end of Chapter 28 Julian writes that:

> out of his great courtesy [God] sets aside all our blame, and he regards us with compassion and pity as children, innocent and guileless. (BW, LT 28)

This experience of not finding any blame in God was problematic for Julian because it directly contradicted how she felt in herself – ashamed and blameworthy – and what she was taught in the Church, that we are in fact blameworthy for our sins. This contradiction simmers through the *Revelations*, and after some serious rumblings in Chapters 45 and 46, Julian faces it squarely in Chapter 50 as she imagines herself addressing God:

> 'Good Lord, I see that you are very truth, and I know truly that we sin grievously all the time and are greatly to blame. And I can neither stop being conscious of this truth nor see you blame us in any way. How may that be?' For I knew *by the common teaching of Holy Church*, and *by my own feeling*, that the blame for our sins weighs upon us continually, from the first man until the time that we come up into heaven. Then it was this that I marvelled at, that I saw our Lord God blaming us no more than if we were as pure and as holy as angels are in

heaven. And between these two contrary things my reason was greatly afflicted by my blindness, and could have no rest for fear that his blessed presence should pass from my sight. (BW, LT 50, emphasis mine)

Julian's affliction was in feeling caught between opposing truths, all of which she owed her loyalty to: the truth of her mystical experience of there being no blame in God, the truth of her experience of feeling blameworthy, and the truth of the teaching of the Church about sin and blame.

> If I take it in this way – that we are not sinners nor blame-worthy – it seems as though I should be in error and fail to recognize this truth. And if it be so that we are sinners and to blame, good Lord, how may it be then that I cannot see this truth in you, who are my God, my creator, in whom I desire to see all truths? (BW, LT 50)

Furthermore, being unable to see blame in God is disorientating to Julian, not only because of the inner contradiction this causes, but because it seems to undercut her basic moral compass – feeling blame for wrongdoing was, for Julian, a way of knowing that something is in fact wrong to do and thus a guide for moral action:

> I need to know, as it seems to me, if I am to live here, in order to recognize good and evil, so that through reason and grace I can tell them apart more clearly and love goodness and hate evil. (BW, LT 50)

A Mysterious Parable of a Lord and a Servant

In Chapter 51 of her *Revelations*, Julian presents us with what she calls a wonderful visual parable of 'a lord who has a servant', a parable that she felt was given to her by God in response to her inner conflict about blame, and which is arguably the centrepiece of the *Revelations*. Julian says:

[O]ur courteous Lord answered by showing in a mysterious, veiled way a wonderful parable of a lord who has a servant, and gave me insights towards my understanding of both [the lord and the servant]. (BW, LT 51)

Strikingly, this 'parable' given to Julian does not appear in the version of the *Revelations* that Julian composed soon after she had the mystical experiences, yet it appears to have been part of that original experience. Julian tells us that she meditated on this parable for 20 years before writing about it, and found that it captured something essential about the *Revelations* as a whole. In Chapter 51, Julian leads us through several layers of interpreting the parable, beginning with a description of what she saw.

The Parable Described

Her description of the parable is visually commanding. Julian says:

> I saw two persons in bodily likeness, that is to say, a lord and a servant; and with that God gave me spiritual understanding. The lord sits in solemn state, in rest and in peace; the servant stands by respectfully in front of his lord, ready to do his lord's will. The lord looks at his servant very lovingly and kindly, and he gently sends him to a certain place to do his will. (BW, LT 51)

We do well to notice the adverbs and adverbial clauses. The lord sits *solemnly, in rest and peace*. The servant stands *respectfully*. The lord looks *lovingly* and *kindly*. He sends the servant *gently*. And the servant, Julian says,

> does not just walk but suddenly springs forward and runs in great haste to do his lord's will out of love. And at once he falls into a hollow and receives very severe injury. And then he groans and moans, and wails and writhes, but he cannot rise

nor help himself in any way. And the greatest harm of all that I saw him in was a lack of comfort; for he could not turn his face to look at his loving Lord, who was very close to him and in whom is all comfort; but, like someone who was weak and foolish for the moment, he was intent on his own feelings and went on suffering in misery. (BW, LT 51)

Julian's First Interpretation: We Are the Servant and God Shows Us No Blame

At the first level of interpretation, this parable presents for Julian a picture of our human condition. God is the lord, and we are collectively the servant.

The servant who stood in front of the lord I understood to represent Adam, that is to say, one man and his fall was shown at that time so as to make it understood through that how God regards any man and his fall; for in the sight of God all men are one man, and one man is all men. (BW, LT 51)

The parable shows us falling into a spiritual ditch in our very attempt to do God's will, and suffering from this. Julian enumerates 'seven great pains' of the servant in the ditch, from bodily pain and sluggishness to loneliness and a haunting spiritual blindness that amounts to the servant's having almost 'forgotten his own love' for the lord:

[The servant] was hindered and blinded from the knowledge of this will [to love and serve God], and this is a great sorrow … for he neither sees clearly his loving lord, who is most meek and kind to him, nor does he truly see what he is himself in the sight of his loving lord. (BW, LT 51)

Julian says also that she could not see any fault in the servant for his fall, nor any blame in the lord for the servant. The servant is still, as Julian says, 'as inwardly good as when he stood before his lord, ready to do his will', while the lord 'regards him most tenderly in this way ... most gently and kindly, with great compassion and pity' (BW, LT 51). Julian's earlier experience of a God without any wrath or blame is thus reaffirmed. We are not in fact blameworthy and God does not look on us with blame.

Beyond merely not blaming us, Julian even sees the lord 'greatly rejoicing' as a result of our falling, a joy that arises from his intention to reward the servant for all his suffering.

> I saw [the lord] greatly rejoicing over the honourable restoring and nobility to which he would and must bring his servant through his abundant grace ... Then this courteous lord speaks in the following sense: 'See, see, my beloved servant, what harm and distress he has received in my service for love of me, yes, and because of his good will! Is it not reasonable that I should recompense him for his fright and his dread, his hurt and his injury and all his misery? ... [O]therwise it seems to me that I would be ungracious to him.' (BW, LT 51)

Julian finishes the initial experience of the parable in a similar vein:

> And in this an inward, spiritual revelation of the lord's purpose came down into my soul, in which I saw that ... [the lord's] beloved servant whom he loved so much should be truly and blissfully rewarded forever, above what he would have been if he had not fallen. (BW, LT 51)

> And this was a beginning to the teaching revealed to me at this time, through which I might come to know how [God] regards us in our own sin. And then I saw that only suffering blames and punishes, and our courteous Lord comforts and succours; he is always gladly regarding the soul, loving and longing to bring us to bliss. (BW, LT 51)

Julian's Second Interpretation: The Servant Is Jesus

In the many pages of imaginative reflection that follow, Julian provides a second main interpretation of the parable. In this second interpretation, the servant represents Jesus, out of love for us and doing his Lord's will, falling into our human condition in his incarnation. With this, we suddenly have a great doubling up of meanings in the parable, between Jesus and ourselves.

> In the servant is comprehended the Second Person of the Trinity; and in the servant is comprehended Adam, that is to say, all men ... When Adam fell, God's son fell; because of the true union which was made in heaven, God's son could not be apart from Adam, for by Adam I understand all humanity. Adam fell from life to death, into the hollow of this wretched world, and after that into hell. God's son fell with Adam into the hollow of the Virgin's womb ... so as to free Adam through that from guilt in heaven and on earth. (BW, LT 51)

With this double understanding of the identity of the servant, the parable is a striking articulation of divine compassion which, in self-sacrificial love, secures an *unbreakable* connection between ourselves and God. Because of love, and in compassion, God binds Godself to us, and in this love God always follows us into whatever state we choose to be in, or blindly fall into. God, in Jesus, remains open to us, regardless. All that we are and all that we experience is already in God.

When seen this way, the fact that we have done wrong and are responsible for the wrongdoing is still intact from an earthly point of view. But from God's point of view, God sees only God's love in choosing to be one with us in our sin and the suffering it causes. And this choice to love us, while costly to Jesus, is a source of eternal joy and satisfaction in God. For God to blame us would in fact be to put distance between Godself and us, and this is precisely what God refuses to do. Further, God is already in touch with the glory that God is going to give us, as a recompense for what we have suffered in that falling.

Seeing What Faith Is Like: Julian's Way of Faithfulness as a Model for Our Own

Frequently we have seen in our journey with Julian that the life of faith asks us to remain open and compassionate to our own experience and to others, and to God's revelation of Godself in Jesus. In Julian's honesty about the pain and inner contradiction that led to the Parable of the Lord and the Servant, and then in the presentation of the parable itself and her extensive engagement with it, we are witnesses to the life of faith in action in Julian herself.

Allowing Contradiction within Oneself

To begin with, Julian's faith made room for painful contradiction within herself. Julian felt that she had to be *faithful* to her experience of feeling blameworthy, and to the Church's teaching about blame, and to the mystical revelation of there being no blame in God.

A lesser soul would have *broken faith* with one side of this contradiction, just to escape the tension and pain it involved. Julian could, for instance, have renounced her mystical experience as not worthy of concern, something she was in fact tempted to do in the course of the Showings themselves (see Chapter 66). Alternatively, she could have renounced her feelings of blame and the teaching of the Church, and developed what we might call a 'shameless' spirituality, in which any and all behaviour is acceptable. This is also a temptation of which Julian was aware – see for instance her discussion in Chapter 40.

Julian, however, did not break faith with any of the contradicting truths within her. She allowed each of the opposing voices a place and a voice, and it was out of the sustained tension of these different voices that there was, metaphorically, a space in Julian in which the parable could happen.

Likewise, our life of faith is going to create tension in us, tension between what we believe, what we experience and what we might be taught in our faith communities. We might believe, for example, that God is all love and compassion, but our experience might roundly declare the opposite: everything around us might declare that no love is here. We might experience only God's absence in our lives or see only godlessness in others, and yet our faith still declares God's love, presence and active working for the making well of all things. Julian's example instructs us to stay in the tension between these different 'truths' and, in time, to see how they might change one another, or what they might elicit from one another.

The Gift of Insight, Powerful Yet Mysterious

In her case, Julian's willingness to face her inner contradiction squarely *and persistently* allowed the parable to come forward as a mysterious offering, veiled in its meaning at first, but full of power. And, as Julian tells us, not only did the parable linger in her imagination for decades, and inspire reflection, but it also became the subject of a detailed imaginative exercise, as she explored every aspect of the visual appearance of the lord and the servant. She thus allowed the parable to further manifest itself inside her, and meanings to emerge and evolve, as if under the impulse of their own life.

Even if we ourselves are not mystics, such a process of allowing contradicting beliefs and experiences to abide in us can lead to similar experiences where images, words, stories are discovered, or emerge from within, that seem resonant with special meaning and that mysteriously speak to our situation. We feel their depth, we feel their meaning, their total significance to ourselves, even their claim on us, even if we can't at the moment specify what or how this is.

Perhaps the most common example is the image of the crucified Jesus assuming meaning that is powerful but hard to understand, as he hangs in the space between the truth of our experience of suffering on the one hand, and the promise of God's love and compassion on the other. Somehow Jesus, as an image for God, suffering in love to be close to us, manages to touch on, affirm and even include both of those opposite truths. It's not a meaning we can exactly specify, but it brings an inner peace, because in some way it honours – it resonates with – both sides of the contradiction.

Julian's Conclusion about Blame and Love and Practical Christian Living

By the end of Julian's sharing of the parable, the truths that started out in painful contradiction have moved to a different place, not by logical reasoning, still less by an authoritative ruling for one side of the contradiction against the others, but by a deeper feeling for the mystery of compassion that allows each of the different voices to have authority to speak one part of the truth.

In other parts of the *Revelations*, with a curious use of paradox and a deliberate short-circuiting of logic, Julian gives voice to where she ended up in her understanding of the experience of human feelings of blame, of teachings about it, and of blamelessness in God. Regarding how we judge ourselves and how God judges us, Julian says:

> God judges us according to the essence of our human nature, which is always kept united in him, whole and safe without end [thus without blame]; ... man judges on the basis of our changeable sensory being, which seems now one thing and now another ... [a]nd this judgement is mixed, for sometimes it is good and tolerant, and sometimes it is harsh and severe ... and in as much as it is harsh and severe our good Lord Jesus reforms it by mercy and grace through the power of his blessed Passion ... And although these two are thus reconciled and united [through Jesus], yet *both shall be known in heaven without end*. (BW, LT 45, emphasis mine)

And later in the *Revelations* Julian writes something even more compelling:

[I]n falling and in rising we are always inestimably protected in one love; for in the sight of God we do not fall, and in our own view we do not remain standing, *and both of these are true, as I see it, but the sight of our Lord God is the highest truth.* So we are much indebted to God that he wishes to reveal this high truth to us in this life. (BW, LT 82, emphasis mine)

Both ways of seeing are true, and both ways help us to live wisely:

And I understood that while we are in this life, it is most advantageous to us to see both of these at once; for the higher view keeps us in spiritual solace and true delight in God; the other, that is the lower view [that we are blameworthy], keeps us in fear and makes us ashamed of ourselves. But our good Lord always wants us to regard ourselves much more in accordance with the higher view, and yet not to relinquish our recognition of the lower one, until the time when we are brought up above, where we shall have our Lord Jesus for our reward, and be filled full of joy and bliss without end. (BW, LT 82)

What we see in these passages is a deliberate, nuanced affirmation of the different truths that originally had caused such pain for Julian.

Julian's feeling of blame and guilt is assured that, as a feeling of something being wrong, it is true and need not be denied. This is part of our human condition; it is true as a feeling, but is not an indication of our ultimate reality nor how God looks at us.

The teaching of Julian's medieval Church, that we are worthy of blame when we do wrong, is assured that it still has a place in helping human beings take responsibility for their lives, their choices and discerning what is good and bad for us. This judgement is thus welcomed as practically necessary and advantageous, even if the suffering it can cause will need redeeming, like sin itself!

Finally, *the mystical revelation of God's assigning us no manner of blame*, while being pre-eminent as the highest truth, is importantly revealed as not negating the other truths, and as requiring an enormous self-sacrifice in God. Such a higher judgement as Julian sees of God regarding us without blame is possible only because God, in Jesus, is intimately and irreversibly bound to us and suffers with us in love and compassion. That God does not blame us is thus an invitation to a deeper intimacy, a deeper gratitude and, so we might say, a deeper *Eucharist*, based on the sacrifice God made in order to remain open to us without conditions.

Questions for Reflection and Discussion

1   Julian affirms, at the end of all her questioning, that God assigns us no manner of blame. God regards us as innocent, she says, as children, or as the angels. Can you recollect something that you have felt blameworthy for, or guilty about, or ashamed of, something that you think God *should* blame you for? What is it like to let go of that blame, at least a little, or to feel your own blame of yourself but to know that God does not blame you? Does it help to recognize how much it cost God not to blame you – in terms of Jesus' suffering the hurt we have caused?

2   Are you comfortable living into Julian's multi-levelled approach to truth and judgement: that on one level, yes, we need a human judgement that approves some things and condemns others, but that on another level this needs to be taken up into a greater truth where God shows us no blame, but only shows us Jesus and ourselves as infinitely cherished? Is it possible to have these two different viewpoints in yourself at the same time?

3   Do you feel there are contradictions right now in yourself between what you experience and belief in a God of unconditional love? For example, we can often feel resentment towards others who have hurt us, and yet we are told in the *Revelations* that God rejoices in them, loves them, wants to heal them and us. What does it feel like to allow both

truths – your feeling of resentment and anger and the truth of God's love for the other person – to be true in some way? What is it like to live in the middle of that contradiction? Does the image of Jesus crucified help, as you reflect on this?

PART THREE

Julian's Counsel: Wisdom and Imagery for the Journey of Faith

15

A Marvellous Mixture of Happiness and Sorrow

Beginning the Third Stage of Our Journey

In Part One of this book we saw a vision for faith emerging from Julian's first 12 Showings. Julian, and we, were plunged into a series of mystical visions, words, insights and reflections that seemed almost too rich to digest. The critical moment came in Showing 8 when Julian chose 'Jesus for her heaven' in joy and suffering.

In Part Two, Julian critically challenged her faith in God's love on two fronts. How could a God of love have allowed sin and the suffering it causes? And how could a God who shows us no blame be reconciled with Julian's own feelings of being blameworthy, and the teaching of the Church about blame? In both of these questions, Julian felt tension between the truth of her mystical experience and the truth of other authorities. This tension led to the gift of 'all shall be well' and to the Parable of the Lord and the Servant. In Part Two we also saw how Julian developed an understanding of how God redeems us, and about God as the foundation of our prayer.

In Part Three, spanning Chapters 52–86 of the *Revelations*, we turn to Julian's final reflections on themes already begun, with Julian offering practical counsel for the spiritual life, along with the creative development of new imagery for God. Reading this last part of the *Revelations* is a chance to deepen our understanding of key themes in Julian, to enrich these with new imagery, and to ask practical questions. How do we go about being faithful in daily life? What are the most common spiritual pitfalls of which we need to be aware?

God's Five Great Joys in Us

Immediately following the Parable of the Lord and the Servant, Julian breaks out into a recitation of five great joys in God:

> And so I saw [Julian says] that God rejoices that he is our father, God rejoices that he is our mother, and God rejoices that he is our true spouse, and our soul is his beloved wife. And Christ rejoices that he is our brother, and Jesus rejoices that he is our Saviour. There are five great joys, as I understand, in which [God] wishes that we rejoice, praising him, thanking him, loving him, endlessly blessing him. (BW, LT 52)

As multi-layered as Julian's interpretation of the Parable of the Lord and the Servant can be, and as complex as the *Revelations* is as a whole, there is yet, at the heart of it, this simple vision of God rejoicing in us. Julian invites us to claim ourselves as occasions for divine joy, cherishing and tenderness – joy, cherishing and tenderness are, we might say, what happens in God when God sees us.

A Marvellous Mixture of Happiness and Sorrow

Julian was, however, under no illusion that, even with this vision of God's joy, daily life could ever be a simple, sustained rejoicing in God. She experienced, and expected, a fluctuation of feelings and inner states, sometimes feeling consoled and close to God, and sometimes alone and vulnerable to hurt.

Thus, following directly on her recitation of God's five great joys, Julian describes a volatility of experience in herself, similar to what we saw when we reviewed the seventh Showing. Here, however, Julian conceptualizes the alternation between opposite feelings as an alternation between the two different identities that she saw in the servant in the preceding Parable of the Lord and the Servant. Sometimes we experience Christ in us, and sometimes Adam:

> All those who shall be saved, while we are in this life, have in ourselves a marvellous mixture of both happiness and sorrow. We have in us our risen Lord Jesus; we have in us the misery and the harm of Adam's falling. In dying, we are steadfastly protected by Christ, and by the touch of his grace we are raised into sure trust of salvation. And by Adam's fall our perception is so fragmented in various ways, by sins and by various sufferings, in which we are so overshadowed and so blinded that we can scarcely take any comfort. (BW, LT 52)

We fluctuate between Adam and Christ in ourselves, as God touches us with insight but also allows us to fall back into blindness:

> [I]n [God's] goodness [God] opens the eye of our understanding, through which we gain insight, sometimes more and sometimes less, according to the ability that God gives us to receive it. And now we are uplifted into the one, and now we are allowed to fall into the other. And so this fluctuation within us is so baffling that we scarcely know what state we ourselves or our fellow Christians are in, because these conflicting feelings are so extraordinary ... And so we remain in this mixed state all the days of our life. (BW, LT 52)

The main visionary outcome of the parable is thus Julian's celebration of God's joy in us, but the main practical outcome, because we have both Adam and Christ in us, is the truth that we can't live completely within a visionary awareness of God's joy all the time, even if we wanted to. The spiritual and religious life involves a baffling mixture of feelings, fluctuating between happiness and sorrow, consolation and desolation. Julian warns us that this alternation can be so extreme as to be disorientating, certainly confusing. We hardly know who we are in the midst of it: are we the selves that seek to follow Christ and make our lives a place where the world and God's love and tenderness can meet? Or are we wounded creatures who can only cry out from the pain and blindness we are in, and sometimes do things that only cause further hurt? In truth, we are both of these.

The key here is that, for Julian, practising the life of faith does not mean growing out of this fluctuation, leaving Adam completely behind. It does not involve a muting of feelings or a narrowing of experience in order to stay true to an ideal image of the spiritual person. It's not aimed at achieving a *homogenized self*, or a completely detached or dispassionate self. This is not the way it was for Julian, even after her mystical experiences, and it's not the way it is for us.

A life of faith is rather a new richness, breadth and capacity for feelings and experiences, inner and outer, and even a new extremity of the same, because the presence of God allows us to be more welcoming of ourselves and more courageous in our engagement of the world.

Our Intent Is Our Anchor

Julian's practical advice for living well in such a baffling mixture of happiness and sorrow is to anchor ourselves with an *intention* to stay open to God no matter what we might be experiencing. Thus after noting that we are often blinded by suffering, like the servant in the ditch, so that we don't know how to find comfort, Julian says:

> But in our intention we are waiting for God, and trust faithfully that we shall have mercy and grace; and this is how [God] works in us ... [God] wants us to trust that he is perpetually with us ... (BW, LT 52)

Our spiritual anchor is to practise our *intention to stay open to God, and to trust in God's work of mercy and grace, as present and active always for the making of all things well.* Returning to this intention periodically, especially in times of suffering or confusion, is a practical way of enacting and stabilizing our sense of self. It also provides for the ongoing conversation between our experience, our world and God's love that is the heart of a lived faith.

Helpfully, Julian specifies three different ways in which God is with us. She says that God is with us

> in heaven, true man in his own person, drawing us upwards, and that was shown by his spiritual thirst; and he is with us on earth, guiding us; and that was shown in the third revelation, where I saw God in a point; and he is with us endlessly dwelling in our soul, ruling and caring for us, and that was shown in the sixteenth revelation, as I shall recount. (BW, LT 52)

God is present first in the person of Jesus, who draws us to himself in devotional love; second, God is present providentially in all things; and third, God is with us internally, at the centre of all our different feelings and senses, calming, guiding and inspiring us.

However we imagine that God is with us, Julian's advice is always that we should cling to God, should cleave in trust to him, in whatever state we are in:

> I understand two contrary things: one is the wisest action that anyone can perform in this life; the other is the most foolish. The wisest action is for people to act in accord with the wishes and advice of their greatest and supreme friend. This blessed friend is Jesus; and it is his will and his advice that we hold fast to him and adhere to him closely for evermore, in whatever state we may be; for whether we are unclean or pure, his love for us is the same. (BW, LT 76)

Conclusion: Profoundest Self-Acceptance

As a first application of the Parable of the Lord and the Servant to daily spiritual practice, it is striking how the parable allows Julian to welcome our human condition in its glory and in its abasement, to accept it all in the love of God. In the whole of the *Revelations*, Julian models for us a profound self-acceptance, even self-welcoming, and a spiritual practice of intending to remain open to God and close to God in whatever state we are in.

But here is the key: Julian's self-acceptance blossoms naturally from a prior experience of being accepted and loved by another – in her case, by Jesus. Julian comes to self-acceptance across the widest breadth of her experience, from sin to glory, because she knows that Jesus has already seen her accurately, has accepted her entirely and cherishes her becoming. Julian's anchor in life is her intention, *not* to achieve some ideal of spiritual perfection, but to remain open, day in and day out, in suffering and joy, in whatever state she is in, to this friend who sees her truly and loves her unconditionally.

Suggestions for Practice and Discussion

Practising God's Joy in Us

Julian tells us at the start of Chapter 52 about God's five great joys in us. Yet many of us don't feel joy in ourselves. We might be uneasy with ourselves, or embarrassed, or ashamed. In many ways, we are not an occasion of joy for ourselves.

To practise our faith in a God who rejoices in us, a good first step is to recognize how we are feeling now about ourselves. When you look at yourself, are you pleased? Are you dissatisfied, are you annoyed? It is helpful to write your feelings about yourself down, in one or two sentences. Take a moment to pause and then read over the sentence that you have written. Is this accurate? Is this how you feel about yourself now? Is there anything more that needs to be said? Repeat this reflection until what you have written feels right.

The second step is to maintain this sense of how you feel about yourself and to allow, alongside it, Julian's words about God's joy in us:

And so I saw that God rejoices that he is our father, God rejoices that he is our mother, and God rejoices that he is our true spouse, and our soul is his beloved wife. And Christ rejoices that he is our brother, and Jesus rejoices that he is our Saviour. There are five great joys, as I understand, in which [God] wishes that we rejoice, praising him, thanking him, loving him, endlessly blessing him. (BW, LT 52)

This leads to a dual awareness in ourselves. On one side there is an awareness of all that we might feel about ourselves in this moment, and on the other side there is Julian's sense of God's joy in us. Both these senses can exist side by side in us. They might be in harmony, which is wonderful. They might be in contradiction, which is also OK. As we have seen, Julian's kind of faith means staying open to both sides of a contradiction, not collapsing either to escape the tension.

A final step is to imagine how we feel about ourselves as enfolded within God's joy in us, and God's celebration of us as our spouse, friend, brother and mother.

Practising our Intention to Remain Open to God

At various points in our daily life, we can stop and make the intention to be open to God present here and now. We have already seen that for Julian, God is present to us in three different ways: in the person of Jesus, drawing us into himself; providentially in all things; and at the centre of our inner selves. In this spiritual practice, we stop periodically and make an intention to be open to the God who is present in this moment in any of these three ways.

i   We can imagine Jesus as present with us in whatever we are doing or experiencing.
ii   We can imagine God as present in the people and events unfolding around us.

   iii We can imagine God as present at the centre of our-
       selves.

Sometimes, glancing at a holy image or reciting a phrase from
Scripture or a short prayer can buttress our intention.
   What is it like for you to intend to be open to God's presence
here and now? What happens in you as you imagine God present
in these different ways?

16

Already One with God
(Just Not with Ourselves)

A Radical Closeness to God

All through Julian we find traces of radical ideas about our essential closeness to God, a deep resonance in us with God's own life, the hidden presence and action of God in every experience. We have seen also how, as a result of her insistence of there being no wrath in God, Julian was forced to conclude that our way to union with God was through becoming at peace and whole in ourselves: 'When [the soul] is truly at peace in itself, suddenly it is one-ed to God' (JJS, LT 49).

In Chapters 53–59, Julian organizes insights and experiences like these into a coherent, if startling, vision of the human person as irreversibly one with God from the moment of creation, but alienated from this depth in ourselves by suffering and sin, and thus needing Jesus to overcome this alienation and restore us to unity in ourselves.

Articulating this vision, Julian becomes quite theological. But she is not spinning theological theories for theory's sake. Rather, she is attempting, at a much more basic level, to come to terms with her mystical experience of God's loving closeness and her own radical openness to God in the mystery of compassion, and to integrate this with a more ordinary awareness of herself as a confused and suffering creature, who lives contrary to God. She is also attempting to understand Jesus' role in her salvation, an exploration that leads directly into Julian's startling evocation of Jesus as mother, which is the subject of the next chapter of this book.

Julian's 'Godly Will' and the Soul's 'Substance'

Following the Parable of the Lord and the Servant, and inspired by the continual love for God that Julian saw in the servant, Julian announces in Chapter 53 a radical idea. She asserts that each of us has what she calls a 'godly will'.

> [M]y great anxiety was somewhat eased by the loving gracious revelation of our good Lord [in the Parable of the Lord and the Servant]; in which revelation I saw and understood most certainly that in every soul that will be saved is a godly will which never assented to sin, nor ever shall; which will is so good that it can never intend evil, but always intends good constantly, and does good in the sight of God. (BW, LT 53)

Quite differently from how we normally experience ourselves, Julian insists that we have another, godly will that is always willing what God wants and doing good in God's sight. Julian underlines this notion of the godly will with all the authority she can muster, as if she is aware how novel it is.

> Therefore our Lord wants us to know this as a matter of faith and belief, and especially and truly that we have all this blessed will kept whole and safe in our Lord Jesus Christ ... (BW, LT 53)

Here we begin to see where the 'godly will' comes from: it arises out of Julian's experience of the fundamental, inescapable unity of all humanity and Jesus, as well as from Julian's own experience of compassionate openness between herself and Jesus. We share in Jesus' divine life even as he shares in our human experience. The basis of the godly will is thus that there is no clear boundary between us and Christ. Hence we might say that Jesus' will, always in loving response to God, is already flowing into us in a certain way, and moving us to will as he wills, and is a part of our lives as well. To use a metaphor: the divine sea does not just wash up in waves pounding endlessly on our human shore, it actually pours into our human selves, which are like inland seas receiving the flow of divine life and being moved endlessly, within ourselves, by its force, its flow.

Julian quickly broadens this notion of a godly will into something more substantial: an inward depth in ourselves where we are already sharing endlessly in the movement of God's entire life, God's self-presence, God's loving and God's knowing. She calls this inward ground the soul's 'substance':

> ... for all of that kind with which heaven shall be filled must necessarily, through God's righteousness, be so joined and united to him that a substance would be maintained in them which never could nor should be separated from him; and this through his own good will in his endless foreseeing purpose. (BW, LT 53)

The substance of our soul is created by God out of nothing at all, and is joined to God in that creation and endlessly united to God's own life, in a unity that we can do nothing to break.

> And so created nature is rightfully united to the creator, which is essential uncreated nature, that is, God. And so it is that there neither can nor shall be anything at all between God and man's soul. And in this endless love man's soul is kept whole, as the subject matter of the revelations means and shows; and in this endless love we are guided and protected by God and shall never be lost; for he wants us to know that our soul is a life, and this life, through his goodness and his grace, will last in heaven without end, loving him, thanking him, praising him. (BW, LT 53)

Moreover, this spiritual substance is not static, but dynamic; it is an inward life that is loving God, praising God, sharing in God's own life, continually. Earlier in the *Revelations*, Julian described it this way:

God showed frequently in all the revelations that man always works his will, and to his glory, enduringly and unceasingly … man's soul is a creature in God … and [in its substance] it always does what it was made for: it sees God, it contemplates God, and it loves God: and so God rejoices in the creature, and the creature in God, endlessly marvelling. (BW, LT 44)

Where is Jesus in This?

Julian was aware that affirming so strongly a divinely attuned 'substance' in us, always kept safe and whole, regardless of what we do with our earthly lives, might seem to make any faith in Christ or the life of the Church unnecessary. It might appear that, in a sense, we are already saved, by virtue of being created and kept in some kind of union with God; that Jesus was never really necessary to reconcile us with God. Julian argues that this is not the case.

[D]espite this rightful conjoining [between ourselves and God] and this endless union, the redemption and the buying back of mankind is still necessary and beneficial in everything, as it is done with the same intent and for the same purpose that Holy Church teaches us in our faith. (BW, LT 53)

We may, yes, be substantially one with God in 'endless union'. In that sense we can never be separated from God, but Jesus and the necessity of Jesus' incarnation and crucifixion figure in our salvation, and are necessary for Julian in two main ways.

First, Julian understands Jesus' incarnation as a result of the loving God's choice to hold or keep together our blessed inward substance with our outward historical selves, what Julian calls our 'sensory selves'.

And as regards our substance, God made us so noble and so rich that we always work his will and his glory … and from these great riches and this exalted nobility, virtues come to our soul commensurately when it is conjoined with our body, and in this conjoining we are created as sensory beings ... [T]he higher part of our nature is joined to God in its creation; and God is joined to the lower part of our nature in taking on our flesh. And so in Christ our two natures are united. (BW, LT 57)

Jesus, in his incarnation, established the very possibility of our being what we are: physical creatures living in history who can have this substantial depth that is endlessly held open to God. Jesus provides the possibility for our existence in himself, and we are like reflections of him and his reality. Because of Jesus, Julian can affirm that God abides not only in our substance, but fully in our sensory being as well, our physical lives, always changing, always open to suffering.

God is nearer to us than our own soul; for he is the foundation on which our soul stands, and he is the means that keeps the substance and the sensory being together, so that they will never separate ... The noble city in which our lord Jesus sits is our sensory being, in which he is enclosed; and our natural substance is enclosed in Jesus, with the blessed soul of Christ sitting at rest in the Godhead. (BW, LT 56)

Jesus and his incarnation thus makes it possible for there to be creatures like ourselves, who are held open to God at the very base of our being but yet also live physically in space and time. This is the first reason why Jesus and specifically his incarnation is essential for our salvation.

But there is something else. For Julian, Jesus' crucifixion is the logical consequence of Jesus, as God, taking on the totality of our human experience, including our hostile contrariness to God, while staying true to God. Jesus becomes 'sin' for our sake, in the words of St Paul. Jesus allows our violence into himself, to impact on him directly, out of desire to remain open to all that we choose to be and become. And Jesus' suffering of our wrath and violent rejection of God could not be displayed more obviously than it is in the Gospel accounts of Jesus' Passion. The result of God's vulnerability to us in love, coming up against our endemic wrathfulness, is the crucifixion, and it is necessary for our salvation as a logical necessity flowing from God's unconditional loving of us and choice to be with us.

Finally, as we have already seen, the spectacle of love displayed on the cross is the psychological and devotional means for the slaking of our wrath that keeps us alienated from our inward substance where we are already one with God. Our potential hell, as we have seen, is not in being cut off from God, but in being cut off from, because living in ways contrary to, our own substance where God already is. Hell is making for ourselves a reality that is contrary to God's presence and contrary to our own reality as well, and always having to sustain this contrariness. That we are all engaged in this kind of spiritual violence arising out of our hurt, confusion and blindness is something that Julian assumes, and thus that we are all in need of the word of Jesus' cross as a word of love.

Conclusion: Three Kinds of Knowledge

Late in the *Revelations*, Julian suggests that the point of the entire mystical experience recorded in it was to give us three kinds of knowledge.

> It is for us to have three kinds of knowledge: the first is to know our Lord God; the second is to know ourselves, what we are through him in nature and grace; the third is humbly to know ourselves with regard to our sin and weakness. And, as I understand it, the whole revelation was made for these three. (BW, LT 72)

Julian's understanding of the human person as having an inward substance, already united to God, and an outward, sensory being (what we normally think of as ourselves!), and that these two are held together in Jesus in spite of the contrary wrathfulness in our sensory being, establishes the basis for these three kinds of knowledge.

First, the *Revelations* are given to us to know that God is a God of tenderness and compassion who offers Godself endlessly to us, without constraints, for our healing. That love is always offered, always present and is always at work.

Second, God, through Julian, wants us to know what we are through God in nature and grace, which is to say, to know our substantial, inviolate goodness. No matter what we do in our human lives, no matter how hurt, depraved or destructive we become, there remains in us an inward depth of pure innocence, a limpid beauty, open to and participating in God's own life. This is already there, at the base of us, the core of who we are, and God maintains this life in us even as we diverge from it and live contrary to it in our outward selves.

Finally, God also wants us to know ourselves humbly. Although we have a divine substance, we are also hurt and weak creatures, and in God we can safely accept the total reality of how hurt and blind we are. God's love already encloses this, and maintains at enormous cost (the crucifixion) the link between our sometimes wrathful sensory being and God in our inward substance. Furthermore, God provides, again in the crucifixion, the psychological and devotional means for reconciling the two in the slaking of our wrathful rejection of God, self and other. Better, we could say that God's ministry is found in addressing, in Jesus, the fundamental hurt we have in us, and that once this hurt is addressed, the wrath that it generates disappears on its own.

In the next chapter, we will explore further how Julian understands the loving ministry of God to us, not only in healing our hurt, but in encouraging growth and new life, through the metaphor of divine motherhood.

Questions for Reflection and Discussion

Julian's notion of the godly will and the soul's substance arose directly from her mystical experience. Many of us have unexpected moments in life where we experience a seamless unity in

ourselves and all things, often described as 'experiences of God'.
And yet we usually live in ways that are contrary to this kind
of unitive experience. We are often self-centred, anxious, alienated. Julian's notion of our having both a blessed substance and
a sensory being is a way of understanding these different kinds
of experience. At times our sensory being is drawn into resonance with our inner substance, and completely in tune with it;
at times it is in opposition to it, contrary to peace and love.

1 Does Julian's notion of the soul's substance and (usually contrary) sensory being make sense to you? Does it make sense
of experiences of profound calm and unity that happen from
time to time as moments when we are in touch with the
soul's substance where God already is?
2 If you are engaged in contemplative practices such as silence
and meditation, does Julian's understanding of the soul help
you to make sense of these practices as allowing our outward selves a quietness in which they can be drawn into
touch with the inward depth where we are one with God?
3 Jesus, for Julian, makes our human reality possible as
creatures in time open to the full life of God: physical, des-
tined to suffer and die, yet open to God. Does this make you
want to know Jesus more, as the one in whom our integrity
becomes possible again? Does it make sense of going to
church as a place where all of ourselves is welcome in God?
4 In your reading of Julian so far, have you grown more in a
knowledge of yourself in essential goodness? Or in a greater
acceptance of your hurt and weakness? Or in knowledge of
God's love? How would you describe, in your own words,
these three kinds of knowledge to a friend interested in
what you have learned in reading Julian?

17

Our Mother, Who Art in Heaven

Introduction: The Radical Julian

In the late 1980s, in a radical feminist bookstore in a large college town, I found stacks of Julian's *Revelations of Divine Love* for sale. Julian's *Revelations* was there, I believe, because of the feminist discovery of Julian as a spiritual writer who drew on the female experience of motherhood to understand God, and who even referred to God and Jesus as 'our mother'. This was radical in Julian's time, and still is in our own. When the newly elected Presiding Bishop of the Episcopal Church, Katharine Jefferts Schori, referred to Jesus as 'our mother' in her inaugural address in 2006, she was quickly accused of radicalism and even heresy.

From the earliest centuries of Christianity there have been occasional moments, mostly in response to the Gospel accounts of Jesus' comparing himself to a hen who desires to gather her brood under her wings, when maternal imagery has been used to explore how God relates to us. Julian is unique, however, in the extent and complexity of her reflections on God and Jesus as mother. This cannot be dismissed merely as a mystic's imagination running riot. It is a deep affirmation of women's experience, and women's *bodily* experience, as capable of revealing something unique about God, something that exclusively masculine imagery cannot. It also allows for an extended meditation on the manner of Jesus' loving of us.

Motherhood: Womb-like Enclosure, Bodies and Our Birthing into God

Julian's use of the metaphor of motherhood for Jesus springs out suddenly at the end of Chapter 57, in which she reflects on Jesus' enclosing within himself our eternal substance and our 'sensory soul':

> These virtues and gifts [that God wills us to have] are treasured up for us in Jesus Christ; for at the same time that God joined himself to our body in the Virgin's womb he took on our sensory soul, and in taking it on, having enclosed us all in himself, he united the sensory soul to our substance. (BW, LT 57)

Julian's imagination seems to spark at the notion of enclosure, and makes an inspired leap between Mary enclosing Jesus in her womb and Jesus enclosing us in himself. The imagery here is multivalent, but motherhood for Julian is a deeply embodied reality. It is about loving enclosure that allows for a process leading to a new life.

> So our Lady is our mother, in whom we are all enclosed and born of her in Christ; for she who is mother of our Saviour is mother of all who will be saved in our Saviour; and our Saviour is our true mother, in whom we are endlessly born, and out of whom we shall never come to birth. Abundantly, and fully, and sweetly was this shown. (BW, LT 57)

While Julian also reflects on God in general being our mother – in the sense of eternal divine Wisdom having a feminine character (something not unusual in the Judeo-Christian tradition) – she much prefers to talk about Jesus as our mother in his incarnation, labouring in time to reunite us with the substantial inner depth where, as we saw in the last chapter, Julian believes we are already one with God:

Our substance is the higher part [of the soul], which we have in our Father, God almighty; and the Second Person of the Trinity is our mother in nature, in our substantial creation, in whom we are grounded and rooted, and he is our mother in mercy by taking on our sensory being. And so our mother – in whom the parts of us are kept undivided – works within us in various ways; for in our mother, Christ, we profit and grow, and in mercy he reforms and restores us, and, by virtue of his Passion and his death and resurrection, he unites us to our substance. (BW, LT 58)

And so Jesus is our true mother ... All the fair work and all the sweet, loving offices of beloved motherhood are appropriated to the Second Person [of the Trinity, incarnate in Jesus]. (BW, LT 59)

Julian's most extended and vivid meditation on the theme of Jesus' motherhood arrives in Chapter 60, where she draws on the experience of natural motherhood to provide a trove of metaphors for how God in Jesus ministers to us.

Jesus Our Mother: Birthing, Feeding, Consoling and Wisely Rearing Us

The first way that Julian sees Jesus' loving service of motherhood is in the labour of birthing us.

We know that our mothers bear us and bring us into this world to suffering and to death, and yet our true mother Jesus, he, all love, gives birth to us into joy and to endless life – blessed may he be! So he sustains us within himself in love and was in labour for the full time ... And when he had finished and so given birth to us into bliss, not even all this could satisfy his marvellous love. (BW, LT 60)

But Jesus is also our mother in feeding us through the life of the Christian community:

> [Jesus] could not die any more, but he would not cease from working. So then he has to feed us, for a mother's precious love has made him owe us that. The mother can give her child her milk to suck, but our precious mother Jesus, he can feed us with himself – and does, most courteously and most tenderly with the blessed sacrament that is precious food of true life. And with all the sweet sacraments he sustains us most mercifully and graciously. (BW, LT 60)

Furthermore, Jesus as our mother at times consoles and comforts us with spiritual experience, but at other times allows us to fall and be chastised by suffering so that we can mature spiritually:

> The mother can lay the child tenderly to her breast, but our tender mother Jesus, he can lead us intimately into his blessed breast through this sweet open side and reveal within part of the Godhead and the joys of heaven. (BW, LT 60)

> And after this [that is, after we have received consolation and inspiration] he allows some of us to fall harder and more grievously than we ever did before, as it seems to us. And then we, who are not altogether wise, think that all that we have started upon was of no value. But it is not so; for we need to fall, and we need to see this ... The mother may allow the child to fall sometimes and be hurt in various ways for its own benefit, but because of her love she can never allow any kind of danger to befall the child. (BW, LT 61)

A Gracious Reprise: Our Journey of Faith in Our Mother Jesus

As we meditate on each of these ways in which Jesus our mother ministers to us, we discover the most essential themes of Julian's vision of the journey of faith and our spiritual journey wonderfully reprised and deepened. It is best to explore the different ways in which Julian sees Jesus our mother ministering to us in an opposite order to that in which Julian presented them.

Consoling Us and Allowing Us to Fall: Joy and Hurt in the Christian Life

First, as we have already seen in several places in Julian's *Revelations*, our spiritual becoming seems to involve an alternation between consolation and desolation, joy and hurt, security in God and despair in feeling left to oneself. Thus, as the 'child' being mothered by Christ, we will be given consolations and inspirations, and 'glimpses of the Godhead'. But we will also be allowed to fall, to hurt ourselves, as an essential part of our spiritual maturation.

It's best to face this directly: that our spiritual maturation is for Julian no steady ascent to ever greater purity and calm. Having faith, practising faith, will likely involve us in a wider range of feeling and experience, greater joys and greater hurts, because it means being more open to God in God's bliss and, at the same time, to our suffering and the suffering of the world. Furthermore, part of God's loving ministry to us is in allowing us to fall, sometimes grievously, because, as Julian says, there is no other way for us to know by experience God's love and our weakness:

> [F]or if we did not fall, we should not know how feeble and how wretched we are in ourselves; nor should we know so fully our maker's marvellous love; for we shall see truly in heaven without end that we have sinned grievously in this life and – in spite of this – we shall see that his love for us remains intact, and we were never of any less value in his sight ... for strong and marvellous is that love which cannot, nor will not, be broken through our transgressions. (BW, LT 61)

Blessed Food: The Spiritual Gift of the Divine Other

If we are to grow in faith, we also need to be fed. We need nourishment. As a metaphor arising out of physical dependence on food, this need to be fed means that in order to grow in faith we need to receive and take into ourselves new life from outside ourselves. More accurately: we need to take into ourselves what is not already ourselves, and digest this, so that it becomes part of us, fully integrated into ourselves. For Julian, Jesus, as our mother, is himself our food, the divine Other who is not us, and yet who gives himself to us for our spiritual becoming. Jesus does this in the Christian community in diverse ways, culminating in the sacramental rituals of the Church.

Christian community is, to begin with, an experience of other-ness: the people gathered together with us in response to Jesus are not ourselves, they are different from us. Thus, insofar as they are different, are truly *other from us*, and insofar as we welcome them into ourselves as essential to our life in Jesus – that is, insofar as we accept the validity in their being with us in the Church and really welcome them – we are given food for our growth. Others' experience, others' difference, allowed to reson-ate in us empathically, catalyse growth because they demand a broadening of our feeling and sensitivity and also allow us to see our limitations and gifts more accurately. This is part of how Christian community feeds us.

Further, in our life of prayer we open ourselves to hear and fully receive God's word of love, allowing it to speak with author-ity in us. God's word and our lived experience then meet within us, and they begin to interrogate each other. God's word of love is thus gradually 'digested' and integrated into the body of our experience (and vice versa). God's word of love, or for instance the Pauline word of the cross, the scandal of God dying as a criminal and religious outcast, becomes a part of us, changing our experience of ourselves and the world.

Finally, for Julian, it is in the sacraments of the Church, par-ticularly the eucharistic meal of bread and wine, consecrated to be Jesus' body and blood, that we take Jesus' own life, full of tenderness and love and courage and honesty, into ourselves. This does not mean that we ourselves suddenly become completely tender, loving, courageous and honest: there may be considerable discomfort as the life of Jesus sits alongside a very different life of fear and dishonesty and distrust in ourselves. Part of the process of the life of faith is allowing for that discomfort to be there, to feel keenly that lack of alignment between how God is in Jesus and how we are, until how we are can be transformed by him. Christian faith is a lifelong process of our being impacted and changed by the otherness of God's life and God's way of love and truth, so different from ourselves, yet taken into ourselves so that it can change us.

Born Anew through His Labour on the Cross

Finally, we have our spiritual birthing in Jesus, which Julian identifies as happening through his Passion and death. This is the central mystery at the heart of the Christian life of faith. We have already seen how Jesus' Passion is a word of unconditional divine love, compassionate presence, and tenderness meant to slake our wrath. We have also seen how the slaking of our wrath allows our everyday selves, free of that wrath, and of fear and resentment, to be drawn into a greater harmony with our inward depths where we are already one with God in peace and love. At one with ourselves in peace and love, we are suddenly united to God (LT 49). And Jesus our mother, as Julian sees it, 'makes us love all that he loves for love of him, and to be well-pleased with him and all his works' (BW, LT 61).

There is, however, something more here, something in the image of Jesus labouring full term on the cross, suffering in order to birth us into life, that needs a moment of further reflection. As we saw in the last chapter, Jesus' self-sacrificial choice in love is to *enclose* within himself all our human experiencing, even our sin, our violence, our hatred and our dying. Jesus dies as a result of his loving choice to open himself to all of us, all of our human experience, even at its most painful and its most destructive.

What this means is that in Jesus on the cross *everything is already included in him*, and thus, as a result, nothing of ourselves and nothing in world history, not our worst sins, nor most violent betrayals, nor most awful sufferings, needs to be excluded from the redemptive process. The whole of our experience and our reality is already included in him. He has already seen, *experienced* and accepted everything of what we are. Thus, in relationship with him, in his Passion, we are able to face our Passions, and in doing so, even though it can feel like death, we are born to new life as people at least one bit more whole in ourselves.

Conclusion: Our Need for Mothers

Julian did not mean to ignite a feminist revolution in writing of Jesus as mother: to assume this would be anachronistic. It seems rather that her imagination was lit up suddenly with the resonance between Jesus and Mary in imagery of enclosure, and processes leading to new life. It also seems that Julian was blessed with a rich and loving sense of motherhood from her own life. In any case, Julian's example gives us permission to be creative in our own imagining of the spiritual life. God, we might imagine, rejoices in the flourishing of devotional imagination.

Questions for Reflection and Discussion

1 Spend some time reflecting on your experience of being a mother, or having a mother, or of other mothers. Is there something in this experience that speaks to you of God, of the spiritual life? For some, fatherhood is a more helpful image. Are both equally helpful, or not?

2 We have seen how Julian believes that Jesus bears us to new life by suffering everything with us in his 'labour' on the cross. Does it help you to imagine that your suffering is already in Jesus as well, and accepted, as he dies on the

cross? Does this feel like an adequate 'enclosure' in him? Do you want such enclosure in another who shares and accepts all your experience? Does it seem to make your experience sharper and closer or duller and more distant?

3 Julian also sees Jesus our mother feeding us with himself, giving us his divine life as our food. Is there any point in your life – praying with God's Word, or receiving the sacraments, or being a part of the Church – that you would describe as being fed by God, nourished by a gift of life not your own? Can you imagine welcoming God's Word into yourself, to speak in you, to reside in you?

4 Our wise mother consoles us but, Julian says, also allows us to fall into sin and suffering. A lot of the time, we tend to imagine our spiritual and religious life as something we do, as entirely our project, as up to us. What is it like to consider that how we feel, or even our ability *not to sin*, is in some sense not fully in our control, that we are dependent on Jesus for everything? Does this arouse fear, or allow for calm?

18

The Final Showings

Introduction: Two Final Showings

For several chapters, we have walked with Julian through reflections on her experience of God in the Showings. Julian has modelled for us a critical questioning of her own most basic experience of God as love, and shared with us the resultant insights and deepening wisdom. One element of the *Revelations* that might have got lost in these lengthy reflections is the sense of Julian telling us a personal story about what happened to her in May 1373. This autobiographical aspect comes to the fore one last time in Chapters 64 to 68, in which Julian shares with us Showing 15, followed by her brief repudiation of the Showings as 'ravings', a demonic attack that came in her sleep, and final reassurance in Showing 16.

Showing 15: Released from Suffering

In Showing 15, Julian returns to a nearly constant concern: the need for divine comfort in the face of human suffering:

> Before this time I had a great longing and desire as a gift from God to be released from this world and from this life; for I often considered the misery that is here, and the well-being and the bliss that it is to be there. And even if there had been no pain in this life except the absence of our Lord, it seemed to me sometimes more than I could bear; and this made me grieve and yearn intensely, as also did my own miserable state,

laziness, and weakness, so that I took no pleasure in living and striving as it fell to me to do. (BW, LT 64)

God responds to Julian's melancholy with a promise of taking her *suddenly* from all her pain, saying:

'You shall suddenly be taken from all your pain, from all your sickness, from all your distress, and from all your unhappiness. And you shall come up above, and you shall have me for your reward, and you shall be filled full of love and of bliss.' (BW, LT 64)

Suffering will not be taken from Julian, but she will be taken out of suffering, and the distinction is important to her:

It is more blessed for man to be taken from suffering than for suffering to be taken from man; for if suffering be taken from us it may come back again. Therefore it is a supreme comfort and a blessed perception for a loving soul that we shall be taken from suffering; for in this promise I saw a marvellous compassion for us which our Lord has on account of our misery, and a courteous promise of pure deliverance. (BW, LT 64)

Here again Julian experiences God's compassion in Jesus; she feels Jesus' empathy and intimacy and, within that, Jesus' promise to take her from all pain. To this, Julian adds a remarkably vivid vision of a human soul rising out of a bloated corpse:

And at this time I saw a body lying on the earth, a body which looked dismal and ugly, without shape and form, as it were a swollen, heaving mass of stinking mire. And suddenly out of this body sprang a very beautiful creature, a little child perfectly shaped and formed, swift and full of life, whiter than a lily, which quickly glided up into heaven. (BW, LT 64)

As we attempt to live a new life in faith, it is comforting to see that Julian herself struggled with living, and that at times all she

could do was look forward to a future deliverance. Julian suggests that, practically, what we can learn is an ability not to get
completely lost in our suffering even while experiencing it.

> It is God's will that we accept his promises and his comfortings
> as generously and as fully as we can take them. And he also
> wants us to take our waiting and our distress as lightly as we
> can take them and count them as nothing; for the more lightly
> we take them and the less value we set on them out of love, the
> less pain we shall experience from feeling them, and the more
> thanks and reward we shall have for them. (BW, LT 64)

With Julian we gain, not invulnerability to hurt, but the ability to
experience our hurt and remain in touch with something outside
it – a wider soul, capable of welcoming divergent experiences at
the same time. And it is perhaps the devotional knowledge that
we are accompanied in our suffering by another, who sees it and
feels it and promises to take us from it suddenly, that gives us
this ability to both experience the pain of life yet not be engulfed
by it.

It Was Raving! And a Demonic Attack

Following Showing 15, Julian feels compelled to tell us first
about something that makes her feel ashamed, so that we can see
her in her 'weakness, wretchedness, and blindness' (BW, LT 66)
before she relates Showing 16.

The pain of Julian's bodily sickness washed back into her following Showing 15:

> [S]traightaway my sickness came back: first in my head, with a
> sound and a din; and suddenly all my body was filled with sick-
> ness just as it was before, and I felt as barren and as dry as if I
> had only ever had little comfort. And like a wretch I mourned
> and grieved on account of the bodily pain I experienced and
> the lack of comfort, spiritual and bodily. (BW, LT 66)

When she was in this state, Julian was visited by a member of a religious order.

> Then a member of a religious order came to me and asked me how I was getting on. And I said I had been raving today, and he laughed loudly and heartily. And I said, 'The cross that was held in front of my face – it seemed to me it was bleeding hard.' And at these words the person to whom I was speaking was amazed and became very serious. And at once I felt very ashamed and astonished at my carelessness and I thought: 'This man takes seriously the least word I say, yet knows no more of it than that.' And when I saw that he took it seriously and so very reverently, I grew very much ashamed, and wanted to have been confessed ...
>
> Ah, look what a wretch I was! This was a great sin and great ingratitude that I – through stupidity, because of feeling a little bodily pain – so foolishly lost for the time being the comfort of all this blessed revelation ... (BW, LT 66)

Julian discounts her mystical experiences as mere ravings, as if embarrassed by them, and then is ashamed when her visitor takes her seriously.

Comparing this passage with Showing 15, where Julian has just confidently advised us to look past all suffering and take comfort in God, the juxtaposition produces a poignant sense of just how fragile spiritual insight and intention was in Julian, and in us. We can know that, in the compassion of Jesus, we have a way of patiently living with suffering, but then, a moment later, a sudden onset of suffering can drive us away from this very possibility.

Julian, for her part, feels she is cast out from the comfort of the Showings, and it's in this state, perhaps not coincidentally, that she experiences what she interprets as a demonic attack in her sleep, a dream-vision of the devil pawing at her throat, followed on her waking to a stench and sense of fire in the room, which only she notices and not those around her. Frightened by this, Julian clings to the faith of the Church and to her mystical experiences as truly from God. This allows her a measure of peace and calm.

Showing 16: Jesus Enthroned at the Centre of Ourselves

The final Showing, coming directly after this rather horrible experience, comforts and reassures Julian. It is in a way the crowning happiness of all the Showings. She sees Jesus enthroned at the centre of her 'inner self'.

> I saw the soul as large as if it were an endless world, and as if it were a blessed kingdom; and from the properties I saw in it I understood that it is a glorious city. In the midst of that city sits our Lord Jesus, true God and true man, a handsome person and of great stature, highest bishop, grandest king, most glorious lord ... He sits in the midst of the soul in peace and rest ... Through all eternity Jesus will never vacate the place he takes in our soul, as far as I can see; for in us is the home most familiar to him and his everlasting dwelling. (BW, LT 67)

We are the home most familiar to our God, who is homely with us. And in exploring this final Showing, Julian reiterates many of the themes we have already encountered in the *Revelations*: God's loving delight in us, our natural loving delight in God, and how God alone can bring us to true rest.

> This was a delectable sight and a restful revelation, that it is so without end. And to contemplate this while we are here is most pleasing to God and of the greatest advantage to us. (BW, LT 68)

And, as always, such gazing on God makes us like God and brings us peace:

> And the soul that contemplates in this way makes itself like the one that is contemplated and unites itself in rest and peace through his grace. (BW, LT 68)

And finally, as the last moment in Julian's *Revelations*, God reassures Julian of the truth of the Showings and of God's own everlasting care.

> [O]ur Good Lord revealed words to me very gently, voice-lessly, and without opening his lips … and said very lovingly, 'Be well aware now that what you saw today was no delirium, but accept it and believe it, and hold to it, and comfort yourself with it, and trust in it, and you shall not be overcome.' (BW, LT 68)

> He did not say, 'You shall not be perturbed, you shall not be troubled, you shall not be distressed', but he said, 'You shall not be overcome.' God wants us to pay attention to these words … he wishes us to love him, and be pleased with him, and strongly trust in him; and all shall be well. (BW, LT 68)

Put together, Showings 15 and 16 are God's final words of reassurance to Julian. Our lives may involve considerable suffer-ing, but we shall be taken from all this suffering, almost without warning, and it will seem as nothing once it is past. And even though it may seem to us that we will be overcome by suffering, and even though we make ourselves vulnerable to more spiritual pain and threat when we sin, we are always, always, protected by God in love. We will be troubled and distressed, but we will not be overcome. Even in our distress, God is present, inviting our trust and making all things well. Having thus blessed Julian with a vision of Jesus at the very centre of her being, ruling, loving, protecting, guiding, the Showings draw to a close:

> And soon afterwards [Julian says], everything was at a close, and I saw no more. (BW, LT 68)

Questions for Reflection and Discussion

At the very end of her account of her mystical experiences, Julian bids us pay attention to the words, 'You shall not be overcome.' She also says that God 'wishes us to love him, and be pleased with him, and strongly trust in him; and all shall be well'. At this point in your journey with Julian, what would it mean for you to:

1 **Love God more**: Would this have to do with reading Scripture more, or attending to the needs of your neighbour, or making it more a habit to recollect inside yourself, where Jesus already is, and offer God short prayers of love and praise? How can you imagine loving God more in daily life?

2 **Be pleased with God**: Where is there wrath in you? What prevents you from being pleased and satisfied with God, with Jesus, in the here and now? Give this wrath voice. What does it say? What would it say to Jesus?

3 **Strongly trust in him, that all shall be well**: How have you experienced walking alongside Julian, and her invitation to grow in trust that absolutely all things shall be made well? How does this seem to you at this moment? Are you willing to accept this about all your life, or are there parts, in yourself or for others, that still seem outside God's well-making? Give these parts voice. What would they say? What would they say to Jesus?

19

Impatience, Sloth and Despair

Introduction

Following the story of her mystical experiences, Julian offers
several chapters of closing reflections, summarizing aspects
of her teaching and offering advice for practising the kind of
faith that we have seen emerge in her *Revelations*. Most helpful
in terms of practical pastoral counsel is Julian's discussion in
Chapter 73 of two sins of which we need to be most wary, and
intertwined with these in Chapter 74, four fears that we commonly experience in human life. In understanding these 'sins'
and Julian's advice for treating them, we gain a clear sense of
our responsibility for active self-management in the spiritual life.
It is not all blissful gazing on love or sitting in silence; it is also
learning how to recognize spiritually harmful inner processes at
play in ourselves, and how to gently interrupt these so that God's
word of love can slow such processes down, and even reverse
them.

The Two Sins: Sloth and Doubtful Fear

Julian tells us that God showed her two kinds of spiritual sickness from which we are most likely to suffer.

> God showed two kinds of sickness that we have: one is im-
> patience or sloth, because our trouble and our suffering are
> heavy for us to bear; the other is despair or doubting fear ...
> [God] showed sin in general, in which all sin is included, but
> he showed only these two in particular. And these two are the

ones which most trouble and disturb us, by what our Lord showed me, and the ones from which he wants us to be re-formed. (BW, LT 73)

Julian clarifies her audience and suggests causes for these sick-nesses in us:

I am talking of such men and women who for the love of God hate sin and dispose themselves to do God's will. Then through our spiritual blindness and the burden of our bodies we are most inclined to these sins; and therefore it is God's will that they should be recognized, and then we shall reject them as we do other sins. (BW, LT 73)

While destructive anger, or seething envy, or obsessive desires are relatively easy to identify as sicknesses of soul, Julian's focus here is on more elusive inner states that are harder to identify and yet are profoundly destructive to the life of faith.

Impatience and Sloth?

The first sin that Julian specifies, that of 'impatience or sloth', is difficult to understand, since *impatience* and *sloth* as terms sug-gest opposite states of mind: jittery frustration on the one hand and numbing torpor on the other. However, when we think of Julian's frequently confessed longing to be free of the suffering of her life, and her specifying the 'burden of our bodies' as inclining us to this sin, we begin to get a picture of what Julian is talking about.

Life can be a trial. We endure sufferings that are physical, social and spiritual, and when these weigh us down we are 'impatient' because we don't want to endure any more. In other words, we begin to become ever so slightly wrathful against our experiences because of the suffering in them. We have had enough, we don't want it; and although we are still experiencing the suffering, we are rejecting it.

With this incipient rejection of our experience, the torpor of sloth also sets in because when we close down against what we are experiencing, and thus locate ourselves apart from it, we also lose any place in ourselves where we can be authentically open to God. When we lose the capacity to be open to ourselves we lose the capacity to be open to God.

It's not that we renounce our selves, our lives, or our faith openly, we rather just sink into numbing spiritual torpor. Outwardly we might be physically lazy, or we might be physically and mentally frantic, but either way we have fallen away from the most basic practice of faith, as this has emerged for us in our journey with Julian – holding ourselves open in compassionate welcome to ourselves, and others, and God's word of love.

Such spiritual impatience and sloth is a universal experience for those seeking to live a faithful life. We wake in the morning and feel in our bodies the ache of a longstanding illness, or perhaps we wake to the prospect of an impossible workload waiting for us at a hostile workplace, or perhaps to a sense of personal failure or fractured relationships. For these and countless other reasons, a wrath against our experience begins to rise in us, and we grow impatient with our lives and slothful in our faith.

Julian's Antidote

The antidote to this spiritual malaise is, Julian says, the contemplation of Jesus.

> And our Lord very humbly revealed what is most helpful for this [our struggle with the sins of sloth and despair]: the patience that he had in his cruel Passion, and also the joy and the delight that he has in that Passion because of love. And this was shown by way of an example that we should bear our sufferings gladly and wisely, for that is greatly pleasing to him and endless benefit to us. (BW, LT 73)

Julian suggests that, when we find ourselves closing down against our experience, and so losing our openness to God, as described above, we choose to insert into the middle of our relationship with ourselves the memory, the awareness, of Jesus in his suffering and death, and in particular his *patience*. Doing this, we can have a sense of Jesus' willingness to go on being open in compassion and love into the unforeseeable future. Such a sense, of Jesus' patience through long suffering, has the effect of calming and coaxing us to be more open, less wrathful, in relation to our current suffering, our burden, our plight. It's as if we see in Jesus how to be open again to ourselves, and this, in turn, allows us to be more open to God.

A further step, Julian suggests, is to remember Jesus' delight in his Passion. This further invites us to be open to ourselves and to him and to God, not merely in suffering but in joy. Such remembrance of Jesus' delight in the Passion is like a second level of treatment that can create further health in us. We start with his patience, and we move then to his joy.

Thus when Julian says that we 'should bear our sufferings gladly and wisely' and that this is pleasing to God and 'endless benefit to us', she is *not* saying that we should just yank ourselves out of gloom and force a fake gladness on ourselves. Rather, we should invite another, Jesus, the suffering and patient one, into our suffering, and allow his patience and his delight to ease, coax, soothe and open us back to health. We travel back to ourselves through the patience and delight of Jesus.

The Second Sin: Doubting Fear

The second sin that Julian specifies for special care – doubting fear – is closely related to impatience, but has a different cause and only a slightly different treatment. Julian explains what she means by doubting fear, and what she sees as its cause, in the last half of Chapter 73 and in her discussion of it as one of the four fears that we can experience in this life in Chapter 74. Along with the fear of fright, arising from sudden alarm, and the fear of punishment that prompts us to amend our lives, doubting fear is for Julian a kind of self-centredness arising out of our own shame. Julian describes with precision how doubtful fear arises.

[W]hen we begin to hate sin and to mend our ways according to the laws of Holy Church, there still persists a fear which holds us back, through self-scrutiny of ourselves and our sins committed previously, and some of us because of our sins every day; because we do not keep our promises nor keep to the purity in which our Lord has established us, but often fall into so much baseness that it is shameful to see it. And it makes us so sorry and so depressed to recognize this that we can hardly find any comfort. (BW, LT 73)

Unlike the sin of *impatience*, which arises out of suffering, doubting fear arises from shame. It is a kind of morbid self-dramatization which, just like impatience, closes down the possibility of faith because it involves a rejection of ourselves, and it excludes the possibility of God helping us. It may well draw us on to despair. What makes the sin so tricky, for Julian, is that it often masquerades as humility:

[W]e sometimes mistake this [doubting] fear for humility, but it is a reprehensible blindness and weakness. And we are unable to despise it as we do another sin that we recognize, for it derives from our enemy and is contrary to truth. (BW, LT 73)

The treatment for such doubting fear is, once again, first to see that it is happening and then to interrupt the experience of shame with the remembrance of divine love, and even to interrogate ourselves, our shame, with the reality of God's love: do we really believe that God is love and can love all that we are and all that we have done into wellness?

[T]he reason why we are troubled by [these sins] is because of our failure to recognize love ... [God] wishes that we perceive love in all things and rejoice in it. And we are most blind in recognizing this; for some of us believe that God is almighty and may do everything, and some that he is all wisdom and knows how to do everything; but that he is all love and is willing to do everything – there we stop short. And it is this

ignorance that most hinders those who love God, as I see it.
(BW, LT 73)

Conclusion: Living a Faithful Life

There is throughout Julian's spirituality a decidedly contemplative and even a passive feeling; Julian gazes on Jesus as Jesus
unfolds his experience to her, and she is carried along by what
she sees to share in the movement of God's own life. This is
beautiful, and meaningful, but Julian was no fool. She was also
aware of the very human protest and refusals we find in ourselves, and the hardship and pain of life, and that the life of
faith is not a matter simply of being swept up into God's bliss.
God also needs us to take active responsibility for ourselves. God
needs us to practise vigilance and active self-management. When
we find impatience arising in us, when we feel shame drawing us
to despair, Julian counsels us to intervene with our inner process
and bring to mind the patience of Jesus, or gently interrogate
our shame with our awareness of God's unconditional loving.
Such vigilance and self-interventions are our most basic way of
keeping us open to something more than ourselves.

Questions for Reflection and Discussion

1 Are you more troubled by anxious fretfulness, or by despair?
   Julian would suggest they are interconnected, based in a
   similar spiritual reality in which we are closing down ourselves to the word of God's love. Does this seem correct to
   you?
2 Julian returns in these chapters to the notion of God making
   well all things, and encourages us to believe in God's love as
   making well all our sin and wrongdoing. Where have you
   journeyed since your first exposure to this idea in Julian?
   Has this been a major struggle for you? Are you now more
   willing to grant that love can be present, is present and is
   making things well in more of your life, or not?

3   Try to do what Julian suggests in these chapters. Call to mind
    an experience of suffering that makes you feel impatient,
    even angry. Then bring into the middle of this experience
    your awareness of Jesus' patience in his suffering. Does this
    help? Does it shift how you feel?

20

Light and Love in Daily Life

A Revelation of Love, a Journey of Faith

Julian is a mystic of God's love, and her book is just what it says it is: a revelation of God's unconditional love for us. For Julian this love is realized in history in the person of Jesus of Nazareth, God's Word made flesh, and it is active within us in the mysterious working of God's Holy Spirit. Our life of faith, in its bare essence, is a choice to hold ourselves open to this revelation of love in Jesus and Spirit, allowing its working within us, and through us for others.

One of the strangest things that we have discovered in our journey with Julian is that it is not always comfortable or consoling to be open to the love of God. Because God's love is unconditional and unconstrained, it shows up by contrast how conditional and constrained we are and how limited our love is. It highlights how much wrath and fear and hurt we have in us and how this controls us. Most of us, it is true, want to be loving, but only to a limited degree, or within a limited segment of reality, and then to be dismissive and excluding, or at least inattentive, to the rest. This is perhaps the greatest block in most spiritual lives: because we love a little bit, we assume that this is where God is, and become complacent with that. We are happy to think that the Kingdom of God has already arrived. Julian's *Revelations*, when we allow it to interrogate us, pulls apart such complacency. It makes us aware of how different God's way of loving is, and how we habitually run counter to it in our relationships with ourselves, with others and even with God.

The life of faith, as a result, is a lifelong interplay between God's unconditional love and our constrained loving, between God's total honesty and our murky duplicity in which we can't bear too much reality, between God's willingness to see and own everything and our desperate need to deny and distort so much of our experience. Journeying with Julian is learning to see as God sees and love more and more as God loves.

As we end our journey through the *Revelations*, Julian, in the last chapters of her book, does two main things. First, she reflects extensively on the experience of ordinary life lived in faith, using the unexpected metaphor of penance to describe ordinary living. Second, she presents us with a closing meditation on three blissful properties in God – light, love and life – and, as Julian does so, it's as though she disappears from our sight into this light and love and life.

Reinventing Penance as Our Lived Surrender to God

Julian, surprisingly, uses the metaphor of 'penance' to describe ordinary human life. Denoting life itself as our penance is not immediately attractive, nor does it sound particularly joyful, yet God advises Julian to recognize the penance she is in constantly, just in being alive:

> I want you wisely to recognize your penance, which you are in constantly, and humbly to accept it as your penance, and then you will truly see that your whole life is a profitable penance. (BW, LT 77)

Julian clarifies that this penance is, at least in part, that of longing without satisfaction for God:

> [God] looks upon us so tenderly that He sees all our living here to be penance. The natural yearning in us for Him is a lasting penance in us, which penance He produces in us and mercifully helps us to bear it. (JJS, LT 81)

The medieval era was rife with people imposing penances on themselves to placate what they understood as the wrath of God, but for Julian there is no divine wrath to be placated, and no need to impose special sufferings on ourselves. If penance is going to placate anything, it is going to be our wrathfulness, our refusal of God. In taking up the metaphor of penance to talk about daily life, Julian is thus viewing daily life, with its inevitable suffering, as part of God's loving gift to us, the arena and the means of our healing and transformation. Lived in the right way, daily life can be the means by which we overcome our blindness and resistance to love. It can be the royal road to a deeper life in God.

The metaphor of penance is thus useful as a way of evoking an active return and wide embrace of life, consciously going back to life now and choosing it as widely and fully as possible, as God's ministry to us and the medium for our surrender in return.

> For the penance which people impose upon themselves was not revealed to me; ... but it was revealed especially and exaltedly, and in a most loving manner, that we should humbly and patiently bear and suffer the penance which God himself gives us, in recalling his blessed Passion; for when we bear in mind his blessed Passion, with pity and love, then we suffer with him as his friends did who saw it. (BW, LT 77)

Julian thus counsels humility, trust and patience in accepting the ordinary life we have right in front of us, and keeping Jesus' Passion in mind as we do so. In this way, we become true friends of Christ.

Where We End Is Our Beginning

> What we call the beginning is often the end
> And to make an end is to make a beginning.
> The end is where we start from.
> (T. S. Eliot, 'Little Gidding', V, *The Four Quartets*,
> London: Faber & Faber)

The original desire behind Julian's whole spiritual journey, which we saw in Chapter 2 of the *Revelations*, was for her, and so for us, to become true lovers of Christ, compassionate with him, and like his friends who suffered with him in his Passion. In Chapter 3, wavering on the brink of death, Julian realized she did not need an extraordinary visionary experience of the Passion in order to have an intimate and compassionate union with Jesus. Rather, this could happen instead by living with a surrendered heart in ordinary human life. At the very end of her *Revelations*, in her writing about life as penance, Julian returns exactly to this profound starting point, only with much deeper understanding of what it means and what it asks of us.

We become true friends and true lovers of Christ when:

- we live openly and with a surrendered heart in the penance we are in continually, the reality of this present moment; and
- we bear in mind the Passion of Christ as we do so.

Thus faith – that common word bandied about so much in churches and society as whole, but often understood so little – is now, at the end of our journey with Julian, understood clearly and specifically for what it does.

Christian faith holds us open to our experience, the 'penance' we are in, whatever this is, with ever increasing acceptance, which is to say surrender to God. Such faith also holds us open to the word of divine love, uttered specifically in Jesus of Nazareth, as a word of tenderness and truthfulness, courage and self-sacrificial responsibility spoken into world history and into ourselves. And there is a circularity in this process: discovering God's love for us in Jesus, we discover that this love is welcoming of all of us, without conditions, and thus invites us to be more welcoming of all of ourselves, and all of each other, and each moment of life as being where God is both suffering and at work for the making of all things well. Faith makes us compassionately open to ourselves and others, more truthful, and tender even to God's desire for us.

Thus, as a final articulation of all that we have explored, we can say that the life of faith is a sustained openness, even a tenderness, towards ourselves and our inner experience, towards others and the world, and towards God's love in Jesus and the Spirit, so that all these can meet within us, and the process of God's redemptive work can extend further in us, and through us into the world. As Julian says about prayer, such faith is what allows us to become like God in character, in the manner of our living, as each human being is already like God in nature.

In short, we become places where God's love meets the world, and where the world meets God. We can become a lived extension of Jesus' gospel, and part of the completing of Julian's *Revelations* for which she herself prayed:

> This book was begun by God's gift and his grace, but it is not yet completed, as I see it. With God working within us, let us all pray to God for charity, thanking, trusting, rejoicing; for it is in this way that our good Lord wishes to be prayed to. (BW, LT 86)

God as Our Light, Our Life, Our Love

Julian's final meditation on God is on three properties that she says she sees and feels and touches(!) in God: light, life and love.

> I received in some measure, touch, sight, and feeling [Julian says] of three properties of God in which the strength and significance of the revelation consists; and they were seen in every revelation ... The properties are these: life, love, and light. In life there is marvellous familiarity, in love there is noble courtesy, and in light there is endless kindness. (BW, LT 83)

Life, love, light. Marvellous familiarity and noble courtesy, all in endless kindness: this is Julian's God. And our faith comes from this God into us, holding open that space in us that remains welcoming to the full range of our human experience, sometimes good and sometimes bad, along with the revelation of God's love, light and life in Jesus.

> Our faith is a light, coming naturally from our endless day, which is our father, God; and in this light our mother, Christ, and our good Lord, the Holy Spirit, lead us in this passing life. This light is apportioned with discretion, standing by us in the night according to our need. The light is the cause of our life, the night is the cause of our pain and of all our woe ... I saw and understood that our faith is our light in our night – which light is God, our endless day. (BW, LT 83)

And eventually, in heaven, our faith will give way to clear sight of the mysteries of God, which will allow for unqualified affirmation of all things and unqualified surrender to God's life.

> And therefore when the judgement is given, and we are all brought up above, we shall then clearly see in God the mysteries which are now hidden from us. Then none of us will be moved to say in any way, 'Lord, if it had been like so, it would have been very good'; but we shall all say with one voice, 'Lord, blessed may you be, for it is so, and it is well ...' (BW, LT 85)

Julian tells us, in the very last chapter of her *Revelations*, that she wondered for 15 years about God's meaning in giving her the *Revelations*, and God gave her the following as a final assurance:

> 'Do you want to know your Lord's meaning in [these revelations]? Be well aware: love was his meaning. Who showed you this? Love. What did he show you? Love. Why did he show it? For love. Hold fast to this, and you will know and understand more of the same; but you will never understand nor know anything else from this for all eternity.' ... [I]n this love our life is everlasting. (BW, LT 86)

These are very nearly the final words of the *Revelations*. They are for us, Julian's readers, however, also a kind of benediction, a blessing for us on a new journey, the one each of us is about to begin as we step into the moment unfolding in front of us. As we end our journey with Julian in her *Revelations*, we start our journey in the life of faith, lived with God and with all that is right in front of us. Blessed may God be.

Resources for Further Reading

Julian of Norwich in the Middle English

Baker, Denise, *The Showings of Julian of Norwich*, Norton Critical Edition, London: Norton, 2005.

Watson, Nicholas and Jacqueline Jenkins, *The Writings of Julian of Norwich: A Vision Showed to a Devout Woman and A Revelation of Love*, University Park, PA: Pennsylvania State University Press, 2006.

Modern English Translations of Julian

Windeatt, Barry, *Revelations of Divine Love*, Oxford World's Classics, Oxford: Oxford University Press, 2015.

Swanson OJN, The Revd John-Julian, *A Lesson of Love: The Revelations of Julian of Norwich*, Brewster, MA: Paraclete Press, 2016. *The quotations in the present book are taken from the original edition of this translation (London: Darton, Longman & Todd, 1988).*

del Mastro, M. L., *The Revelation of Divine Love Made to Dame Julian of Norwich*, Triumph Books, 1994.

Spearing, Elizabeth, *Revelations of Divine Love*, Penguin Classics, London: Penguin, 1998.

Theological and Spiritual Commentaries on Julian

Abbott, Christopher A., *Julian of Norwich: Autobiography and Theology*, Woodbridge: D. S. Brewer, 1999.

Bauerschmidt, Frederick C., *Julian of Norwich and the Mystical Body Politic of Christ*, Notre Dame, IN: Notre Dame Press, 1999.

Frykholm, Amy, *Julian of Norwich: A Contemplative Biography*, Brewster, MA: Paraclete Press, 2010.

Gatta, Julia, *Three Spiritual Directors for Our Time: Julian of Norwich, The Cloud of Unknowing, Walter Hilton*, Cambridge, MA: Cowley Publications, 1987.

Hide, Kerrie, *Gifted Origins to Graced Fulfillment: The Soteriology of Julian of Norwich*, Collegeville, MN: Liturgical Press, 2001.

Jantzen, Grace J., *Julian of Norwich: Mystic and Theologian*, New York: Paulist Press, 2000.

Llewelyn, Robert, *With Pity Not With Blame: Contemplative Praying with Julian of Norwich and The Cloud of Unknowing*, London: Canterbury Press, 2013.

Meninger, William, *Julian of Norwich: A Mystic for Today*, Great Barrington, MA: Lindisfarne Books, 2010.

Rolf, Veronica Mary, *Julian's Gospel: Illuminating the Life and Revelations of Julian of Norwich*, Maryknoll, NY: Orbis, 2013.

Turner, Denys, *Julian of Norwich, Theologian*, London: Yale University Press, 2011.

Upjohn, Sheila, *Why Julian Now? A Voyage of Discovery*, Norwich: Friends of Julian of Norwich, new edition 2014.

Contemplative Prayer and Practice

Bourgeault, Cynthia, *Centering Prayer and Inner Awakening*, Cambridge, MA: Cowley Publications, 2004.

Keating, Thomas, *Open Mind, Open Heart*, London: Bloomsbury, 20th Anniversary edition 2006.

Llewelyn, Robert, *A Doorway to Silence: Contemplative Use of the Rosary*, London: Darton, Longman & Todd, 1986.

Main, John, *Moment of Christ: The Path of Meditation*, London: Darton, Longman & Todd, 1984.

Pennington, M. Basil, *Centering Prayer: Renewing an Ancient Christian Prayer Form*, Garden City, NY: Image, 1982.

Other Authors Mentioned in this Book

Anonymous, *The Cloud of Unknowing*, ed. William Johnston, London: Fount, 1997.

Burrows, Ruth, *Guidelines for Mystical Prayer*, London: Sheed & Ward, 1976.

de Caussade, Jean-Pierre, *The Joy of Full Surrender*, Brewster, MA: Paraclete Press, 2008.

Dostoevsky, Fyodor, *The Brothers Karamazov*, New York: Farrar, Straus & Giroux, 2002.

Eliot, T. S., *Collected Poems 1909–1962*, London: Faber & Faber, reset edition 2002.

John of the Cross, *The Collected Works of John of the Cross*, Washington, DC: ICS Publications, 2010.

Lewis, C. S., *God in the Dock*, Grand Rapids, MI: Eerdmans, new edition 2014.

Meister Eckhart, *Selected Writings*, trans. Oliver Davies, London: Penguin, 1994.

Tolle, Eckhart, *The Power of Now: A Guide to Spiritual Enlightenment*, Vancouver, BC: Namaste, 2004.